THE LATIN POETRY
OF GEORGE HERBERT

THE LATIN POETRY

A BILINGUAL EDITION

OHIO UNIVERSITY PRESS, ATHENS, OHIO

OF GEORGE HERBERT

translated by MARK McCLOSKEY
and PAUL R. MURPHY

Introduction

Since we are used to Herbert's *The Temple,* where we see
him in his spiritual conflicts and at his devotions, the youthful satire in the *Musae Responsoriae,* the ardent "Baroque"
sense of guilt in the *Passio Discerpta,* and the sly didacti-
cism in the *Lucus* surprise us, as do the *Memoriae Matris
Sacrum* with its Petrarchan grief, and the *Alia Poemata
Latina* with its unbounded flattery. Herbert's Latin verse
is not only in the tradition of the Anglo-Latin poetry of his
time, but it also reveals significant and little-known sides
to his character and style.

The tradition itself springs from the earlier sixteenth century, when the classical forms revived by the Renaissance
began to replace medieval forms, chiefly by means of the
public schools, Westminster and Eton in particular, and
Thomas More's popular translations from the *Greek Anthology.* Furthermore the humanists, More among them,
with their emphasis on religion and education, made the
moral and didactic epigram the chief form of the day.
When the Elizabethan Age arrived, literary interest grew,
and the erotic epigrams of Catullus and Martial, the Ovid-
ian elegy and amatory epistle, the Virgilian pastoral, and
the Petrarchan convention of melancholy and unrequited
love in a pastoral setting became the fashion, as in Herbert's time did the epigram *per se.*

The specific mark of this form was its brevity, as is to be
seen in varying degrees in all the sections of Herbert's verse

here, especially in the *Passio Discerpta* and the *Lucus*. Otherwise the epigram was a vague form using a variety of meters, especially the elegiac couplet. Its techniques— apostrophes, initial questions, quoted conversations, colloquialisms (all inherited from Martial), as well as puns, paradoxes, parallel incongruities, and proverbs ingeniously turned—were not uniquely its own, nor were its subjects, which included addresses and commemorations (*Memoriae Matris Sacrum, Alia Poemata Latina*), moral platitudes and satire (*Musae Responsoriae, Lucus*). Its sources were the *Greek Anthology,* the brief love poems of Ovid and Catullus, and the epigrams of Martial.

The satiric and sacred epigram form special categories in the genre. We see the first, especially its strong polemic side, in the *Musae,* where Herbert ridicules his Puritan antagonist and defends Anglican rites and usages. The witty and passionate rebukes of vice in the *Lucus* are also a feature of the satiric epigram. The second kind of epigram—the sacred—was often in the early seventeenth century based on scriptural themes and liturgical feastdays; thus the epigrams in the *Passio* follow the events of the passion of Christ, while the religious stress and biblical sources of much of the *Lucus* display its partially "sacred" character.

Most of the poems of the *Memoriae* and the *Alia* are too long to be considered epigrams in the strict sense. The *Memoriae* is most noteworthy for its Petrarchan overtones, for its mourning "lover" and its pastoral setting, and the *Alia* for its hyperbolic flattery.

In any case, Herbert's Latin verse, in its various subjects, techniques and forms, follows and contributes brilliantly to the tradition of Anglo-Latin poetry in his day.

With regard to the translations, they have been prepared

for the enjoyment and convenience of those interested in Herbert and his work. The sides to his style and character revealed in his Latin verse have seldom been noted before, and it is this fact which led us to undertake the project.

For the scholar and the critic we took care to be exact in rendering Herbert's imagery and usage, consulting the scriptural and classical sources from which they derive. For the general reader, we used free verse forms, paying close attention to contemporary idiom, and trying to capture the general flavor of Herbert's rhythms as shown by the overall tone and construction of each poem. We have explained obscure references having to do with Herbert's own day or to antiquity in the notes.

As an example of our method of translation in making well note verse 4 of Poem *XIII, Bonus Civis,* of the *Lucus.* Speaking of the blessings which *Humilitas* confers upon good men, Herbert concludes: *Suamque in aliis possidet prudentiam:* literally, "And she possesses her wisdom in others." Herbert is apparently thinking of Matthew 11.19, "wisdom is justified by her deeds" (*variant reading,* children), and Luke 7.35, "wisdom is justified by all her children." We have therefore translated, "She shows / Her prudence through another's acts."

Finally we should like to thank Professor Edgar Whan of the English Department of Ohio University for his fine interest and help in the early stages of these translations, and also thank the Oxford University Press for its permission to print the Latin text, as well as F. E. Hutchinson for his arrangement of the text and for his helpful notes.

Mark McCloskey
and Paul R. Murphy

Index Capitum

Contents

THE LATIN POETRY
OF GEORGE HERBERT

Georgii Herberti Angli Musae Responsoriae ad Andreae Melvini Scoti Anti-Tami-Cami-Categoriam

Augustissimo Potentissimóque Monarchae
Iacobo, D.G. Magnae Britanniae,
Franciae, et Hiberniae Regi,
Fidei Defensori etc. Geo. Herbertus

Ecce recedentis foecundo in littore Nili
   Sol generat populum luce fouente nouum.
Antè tui, *CAESAR,* quàm fulserat aura fauoris,
   Nostrae etiam Musae vile fuere lutum:
Nunc adeò per te viuunt, vt repere possint,   5
   Síntque ausae thalamum solis adire tui.

Illustriss. Celsissimóque Carolo,
Walliae, et Iuuentutis Principi

Quam chartam tibi porrigo recentem,
Humanae decus atque apex iuuentae,

The Englishman George Herbert's Poems in Response to the Scotsman Andrew Melville's Con-Oxford-Cambridge-Accusations [1]

To James, Most Venerable and Strongest of
Monarchs, by the Grace of God
King of Great Britain, France, and Ireland,
Defender of the Faith, George Herbert

Watch how the sun on the mud
Of the Nile ebbing away,
Pushes up with its light a fresh
Nation. Caesar, before the light
Of your grace and attention opened to me,
My Muse too was vile mud:
But now, because of you, she is alive,
She can creep along, and has the nerve
To step up where you are the sun.

To the Most Glorious and Eminent Charles,
Prince of Wales, Prince of Youth

As I hand this fresh manuscript to you,
You the honor and the excellence of youth,

Obtutu placido benignus affles,
Namque aspectibus è tuis vel vnus
Mordaces tineas, nigrásque blattas,   5
Quas liuor mihi parturit, retundet,
Ceu, quas culta timet seges, pruinas
Nascentes radij fugant, vel acres
Tantùm dulcia leniunt catarrhos.
Sic o te (iuuenem, senémue) credat   10
Mors semper iuuenem, senem Britanni.

Reuerendissimo in Christo Patri
ac Domino, Episcopo Vintoniensi, etc.

Sancte Pater, coeli custos, quo doctius vno
    Terra nihil, nec quo sanctius astra vident;
Cùm mea futilibus numeris se verba viderent
    Claudi, penè tuas praeterière fores.
Sed properè dextréque reduxit euntia sensus,   5
    Ista docens soli scripta quadrare tibi.

Please be lenient to it:
For one glance from you will dull
The bites of bookworms, black roaches,
Which envy puts on me.
Just as the beams of morning welling up
Rout the cold the planted wheatfield fears,
One glance from you as much relieves
As bad coughs sweet medicines relieve.
So may to you, young or old,
Death credit youth,
The English people age.

To His Excellency Our Father and Lord in Christ, the Bishop of Winchester

Holy father, watchman of heaven,
Whose learning none on earth can equal,
Whose matchless holiness the stars
Are witness to, when my words saw themselves
Closed up in an empty music,
They kept on past your door.
But sense, quick, sly, caught them
As they went by, and brought them back,
Illustrating that these compositions
Belong to you alone.

Pro Disciplina Ecclesiae Nostrae Epigrammata Apologetica

I. Ad Regem
Instituti Epigrammatici ratio

Cum millena tuam pulsare negotia mentem
   Constet, & ex illâ pendeat orbis ope;
Ne te productis videar lassare Camoenis,
   Pro solido, CAESAR, carmine frusta dabo.
Cùm tu contundis *Catharos,* vultúque librísque,   5
   Grata mihi mensae sunt analecta tuae.

II. Ad Melvinum

Non mea fert aetas, vt te, veterane, lacessam;
   Non vt te superem: res tamen ipsa feret.
Aetatis numerum supplebit causa minorem:
   Sic tu nunc iuuenis factus, egóque senex.
Aspice, dum perstas, vt te tua deserat aetas,   5

Epigrams in Defense of the Discipline of Our Church

1. To the King:
The reason for a project of epigrams

Since a host of things
Dilates your mind, and the world
Hinges on its influence,
And lest I seem to tax you
With tiring verses,
I shall give to you, Caesar,
Not one but several songs.
When you beat down the Puritans
With your looks and learning,
The crumbs of your table
Are precious to me.

2. To Mr. Melville

It's not my age that lets me
Make war on you, a veteran,
And not my age that lets me
Beat you down: the case
Will force me to it: my cause

Et mea sint canis scripta referta tuis.
Ecce tamen quàm suauis ero! cùm, fine duelli,
  Clauserit extremas pugna peracta vices,
Tum tibi, si placeat, fugientia tempora reddam;
  Sufficiet votis ista iuuenta meis.   10

III. *Ad eundem in monstrum vocabuli* *Anti-Tami-Cami-Categoria*

O Quàm bellus homo es! lepido quàm nomine fingis
  Istas *Anti-Tami-Cami-Categorias*!
Sic Catharis noua sola placent; res, verba nouantur:
  Quae sapiunt aeuum, ceu cariosa iacent.
Quin liceat nobis aliquas procudere voces: 5
  Non tibi fingendi sola taberna patet.
Cùm sacra perturbet vester furor omnia, scriptum
  Hoc erit, *Anti-furi-Puri-Categoria*.
Pollubra vel cùm olim damnâris Regiâ in arâ,
  Est *Anti-pelvi-Melvi-Categoria*.   10

Will feed my lesser age:
Now you are thus
The youth, and I the elder man.
Observe how, while you persist,
Your age forsakes you;
What I write has fed
On your grey hair.
And yet see how gentle
I shall be! When at the end
Of the war, peace
Shall have put an end to the final
Back and forth of battle,
Then, if you like,
I shall give back to you
Your lost years and take
—My prayers' reward—your youth.

3. *To the same: On the monstrosity of the title, Con-Oxford-Cambridge-Accusations*

O what a beguiling fellow you are! With what a
Pretty name you shape those *Con-Oxford-Cambridge-*
        Accusations!
For only fads are pleasing to the Puritans;
Words and ways of doing things are changed.
Things that smacked of age he left alone
As though they'd soured. Well, let us also
Hammer out some words; you're not the only one
With access to a smithy. Since your anger
Disorients all sacred things, this will be written:
Con-Raging-Puritan-Accusations. Or since you once

IV. *Partitio Anti-Tami-Cami-Categoriae*

Tres video partes, quò re distinctiùs vtar,
   Anticategoriae, Scoto-Britanne, tuae:
Ritibus vna Sacris opponitur; altera Sanctos
   Praedicat autores; tertia plena Deo est.
Postremis ambabus idem sentimus vterque;   5
   Ipse pios laudo; Numen & ipse colo.
Non nisi prima suas patiuntur praelia lites.
   O bene quòd dubium possideamus agrum!

V. *In metri genus*

Cur, vbi tot ludat numeris antiqua poesis,
   Sola tibi Sappho, femináque vna placet?
Cur tibi tam facilè non arrisêre poetae
   Heroum grandi carmina fulta pede?
Cur non lugentes Elegi? non acer Iambus?   5
   Commotos animos rectiùs ista decent.
Scilicet hoc vobis proprium, qui puriùs itis,
   Et populi spurcas creditis esse vias:

Condemned ablutions on the King's altar, it is
Con-Ablution-Melville-Accusations.

4. On the divisions of the Con-Oxford-Cambridge-Accusations

Anglo-Scot, I note three parts
So I may more precisely deal with
Your *Anti-Accusations*' meat:
One part opposes sacred ritual;
The second praises sacred authors;
The third is full of God. About the latter two
Our minds are in accord: I also praise
Holy men; I, too, worship God.
The first contentions only lend themselves
To disagreement. It is good that we
Take up positions on a doubtful field.

5. On the type of meter

Though classic poetry frolics
In so many different meters,
Why does only Sappho
Tickle you, one lady only?
Why have the poets' ditties
Backed by grand heroic meters
Flirted so little with you?
What's wrong with dolorous
Elegiacs, acrid iambics?

Vos ducibus missis, missis doctoribus, omnes
  Femineum blandâ fallitis arte genus: 10
Nunc etiam teneras quò versus gratior aures
  Mulceat, imbelles complacuêre modi.

VI. De Laruatâ Gorgone

Gorgona cur diram laruásque obtrudis inanes,
  Cùm propè sit nobis Musa, Medusa procul?
Si, quia felices olim dixêre poetae
  Pallada gorgoneam, sic tua verba placent.
Vel potiùs liceat distinguere. Túque tuíque 5
  Sumite *gorgoneam,* nostráque *Pallas* erit.

VII. De Praesulum fastu

Praesulibus nostris fastus, *Melvine,* tumentes
  Saepiùs aspergis. Siste, pudore vacas.
An quod semotum populo laquearibus altis

The former are more fitting
For addled minds, the latter for
You who live in greater cleanliness,
Believing the ways of the people unclean.
Quits with leaders, quits with teachers,
All of you
Take women in with flattery's craft.
So now you've adopted
Pacifist meters, so more delicious
Verses may lull a delicate ear.

6. On the bewitched Gorgon

Why do you intrude dark
Gorgons and ghosts that are nothing
When the Muse is near to us,
Medusa far off? If it's because,
As sweet poets said of old, Pallas
Is Gorgon-faced,[2]
Then your words are good. Let us
Each take a share instead. You
And your friends take Gorgon's visage, Pallas
Will be ours.

7. On the pride of the bishops

Quite often, Mr. Melville,
You accuse our bishops
Of puffed up pride.

Eminet, id tumidum protinus esse feres?
Ergo etiam Solem dicas, ignaue, superbum,   5
    Qui tam sublimi conspicit orbe viam:
Ille tamen, quamuìs altus, tua crimina ridens
    Assiduo vilem lumine cingit humum.
Sic laudandus erit nactus sublimia Praesul,
    Qui dulci miseros irradiabit ope.   10

VIII. *De geminâ Academiâ*

Quis hìc superbit, oro? túne, an Praesules,
    Quos dente nigro corripis?
Tu duplicem solus Camoenarum thronum
    Virtute percellis tuâ;
Et vnus impar aestimatur viribus,   5
    Vtrumque sternis calcitro:
Omnésque stulti audimus, aut hypocritae,
    Te perspicaci atque integro.
An rectiùs nos, si vices vertas, probi,
    Te contumaci & liuido?   10
Quisquis tuetur perspicillis Belgicis

Stop it! You are void of shame.
Or will you call that puffed up which,
Remote from the people, sticks out
From panelled ceilings high up?
So also, buffoon, you would call
The sun proud, who observes his way
With so high a globe:
Yet he, so very high, making
Fun of what you charge,
Surrounds the low earth
With unfailing light. Thus,
The bishop, as one
Who has secured high places,
And who, with his sweet skill,
Will put a light in those who are
Unhappy, will have to be applauded.

8. *On the twin universities*

I ask: Who here is proud?
You, or the bishops,
Whom you tear at with black teeth?
The Muses' pair of royal chairs
You alone with your strength beat down.
One combatant is thought not up
To your power: you
Knock both down with your kicks.
Fools and hypocrites we're called,
While you are smart and pure.
Or is it more correct, if you reverse
The situation, that we are right

Quâ parte tractari solent,
Res ampliantur, sin per aduersam videt,
   Minora fiunt omnia:
Tu qui superbos caeteros existimas   15
   (Superbius cùm te nihil)
Vertas specillum: nam, prout se res habent,
   Vitro minùs rectè vteris.

IX. De S. Baptismi Ritu

Cum tener ad sacros infans sistatur aquales,
   Quòd puer ignorat, verba profana putas?
Annon sic mercamur agros? quibus ecce Redemptor
   Comparat aeterni regna beata Dei.
Scilicet emptorem si res aut parcior aetas   5
   Impediant, apices legis amicus obit.
Forsitan & prohibes infans portetur ad vndas,
   Et per se Templi limen adire velis:
Sin, *Melvine,* pedes alienos postulet infans,
   Cur sic displiceat vox aliena tibi?   10
Rectiùs innocuis lactentibus omnia praestes,
   Quae ratio per se, si sit adulta, facit.
Quid vetat vt pueri vagitus suppleat alter,
   Cùm nequeat claras ipse litare preces?
Saeuus es eripiens paruis vadimonia coeli: 15
   Et tibi sit nemo praes, vbi poscis opem.

And you are stubborn and vicious?
To him who looks through a Belgian telescope,
Through that end which is by custom used,
Things are amplified; but if he looks
Through the other end, all shrinks.
You, who think of other men as proud
(When nothing is more proud than you)—reverse
The lens: for, as things turn out,
You've got the glass
Upside down.

9. *On the sacred rite of baptism*

When before the sacred waters
The soft child is set, you think,
Because the boy is ignorant, the words
Are evil? Don't we likewise trade
In plots of ground? To these, behold, the Savior
Compares the blessed kingdoms of eternal God.
No doubt, if business
Or too few years impede the buyer,
A friend performs the legal part.
Perhaps you will not let the child
Be carried to the waters, and you may
Demand he go up on his own
To the temple gate.
But if, Melville, the child needs another's feet to do so,
Why does another's voice displease you so?
You would more rightly furnish everything
For the milky child, which the age of reason
Of itself accomplishes.

X. De Signaculo Crucis

Cur tanta sufflas probra in innocuam Crucem?
Non plùs maligni daemones Christi cruce
Vnquam fugari, quàm tui socij solent.
Apostolorum culpa non leuis fuit
Vitâsse Christi spiritum efflantis crucem.   5
Et Christianus quisque piscis dicitur
Tertulliano, propter vndae pollubrum,
Quo tingimur parui. Ecquis autem brachijs
Natare sine clarissimâ potest cruce?
Sed non moramur: namque vestra crux erit,   10
Vobis fauentibúsue, vel negantibus.

What won't let another aid
The wailing of a child,
Since he himself can't offer up
Clearly spoken prayers? You are cruel to tear away
The securities of heaven from the young:
May no one be a surety for you
When you cry out for help!

10. *On the sign of the cross*

Why do you put forth
Such evil words
Against the blameless cross?
Miserly devils were
Never more repelled by it
Than your friends are wont to be
By Christ's cross.
Not light the guilt of the Apostles
To have spurned the cross by which the Lord
Breathed out His spirit.
And as Tertullian says,
Every Christian is a fish
Because of the water's cleansing
By which as children we are purified.
Furthermore, who has arms
And does not stay afloat
In the clearest cruciform?
But let us get to the point:
For it will be your cross,
Whether you say yes
Or no to it.

XI. De iuramento Ecclesiae

Articulis sacris quidam subscribere iussus,
    Ah! Cheiragra vetat, quò minùs, inquit, agam.
O verè dictum, & bellè! cùm torqueat omnes
    Ordinis osores articulare malum.

XII. De Purificatione post puerperium

Enixas pueros matres se sistere templis
    Displicet, & laudis tura litare Deo.
Fortè quidem, cùm per vestras Ecclesia turbas
    Fluctibus internis exagitata natet,
Vos sine maternis hymnis infantia vidit,   5
    Vitáque neglectas est satìs vlta preces.
Sed nos, cùm nequeat paruorum lingua, parentem
    Non laudare Deum, credimus esse nefas.
Quotidiana suas poscant si fercula grates,
    Nostra caro sanctae nescia laudis erit?   10
Adde pijs animis quaeuis occasio lucro est,
    Quâ possint humili fundere corde preces.
Sic vbi iam mulier decerpti conscia pomi
    Ingemat ob partus, ceu maledicta, suos,
Appositè quem commotum subfugerat olim,   15
    Nunc redit ad mitem, ceu benedicta, Deum.

11. *On the oath to the Church*

To assent to sacred Articles a certain man
When asked replied: "Oh, gout
Forbids me to!" O true, O lovely answer!
For every hater of right order
Suffers from articular disease.

12. *On the purification after childbirth*

That mothers should present themselves in church
After childbirth
To offer praise's incense to the Lord,
Is not commended.
Though through your mobs the Church,
Agitated by tides within, sails,
Perhaps infancy observed you
Without your mother's hymns, and life
Pressed full hard through neglect of prayer.
But since the speech of childhood is dumb to God,
We believe it evil for a parent
Not to offer praise to him.
If dishes get a daily blessing,
Will our flesh lose the knack of holy praise?
Moreover, for godly spirits it's a gain
—Any chance they have to pour
Prayers from the meek heart.
And so the wife, feeling guilty
For plucking the apple, groans for bearing children
As if she had been cursed; but now, as if blessed,
She rightly comes back to the ripe and mild God
From whom once, when he raged, she ran away.

XIII. De Antichristi decore Pontificali

Non quia Pontificum sunt olim afflata veneno,
    Omnia sunt temere proijcienda foras.
Tollantur si cuncta malus quae polluit vsus,
    Non remanent nobis corpora, non animae.

XIV. De Superpelliceo

Quid sacrae tandem meruêre vestes,
Quas malus liuor iaculis lacessit
Polluens castum chlamydis colorem
       Dentibus atris?

Quicquid ex vrnâ meliore ductum   5
Luce praelustri, vel honore pollet,
Mens sub insigni specie coloris
       Concipit albi.

Scilicet talem liquet esse solem;
Angeli vultu radiante candent;   10
Incolae coeli melioris albâ
       Veste triumphant.

E creaturis sine mentis vsu
Conditis binas homini sequendas
Spiritus proponit, & est vtrique   15
       Candor amicus.

Ergo ringantur pietatis hostes,

13. *On the priestly beauty of the Antichrist*

Not because all things by priests were once
Breathed on with a poisonous breath
Are all things rashly to be thrown away.
If all that evil usage has polluted were removed,
Not flesh or spirit would remain to us.

14. *On the surplice*

Say, what have sacred vestments earned,
Which bad will showers spears upon,
Polluting the pure color of the surplice
With teeth dripping dark?

Whatever drawn up from a finer urn
In strongest light excels, or in honor does,
The mind sees under the select form
Of the color white.

There is no doubt, it is evident, the sun
Is such; the angels from their burning faces
Pour light; the residents of higher heaven
Celebrate in white gowns.

From creatures formed without the use
Of a mind, the Spirit shows to man
These two to follow—the sheep, the dove—and to them
        both
Whiteness is a friend.

So let the enemies of the holy, the sons of night,

Filij noctis, populus malignus,
Dum suum nomen tenet, & triumphat
    Albion albo.   20

XV. De Pileo quadrato

Quae dicteria fuderat Britannus
Superpellicei tremendus hostis,
Isthaec pileus audijt propinquus,
Et partem capitis petit supremam;
Non sic effugit angulus vel vnus   5
Quò dictis minùs acribus notetur.
   Verùm heus! si reputes, tibi tuísque
Longè pileus anteit galerum,
Vt feruor cerebri refrigeretur,
Qui vestras edit intimè medullas.   10
Sed qui tam malè pileos habetis,
Quos Ecclesia comprobat, verendum
Ne tandem caput eius impetatis.

XVI. In Catharum

Cur Latiam linguam reris nimis esse profanam,
   Quam praemissa probant secula, nostra probant?
Cur teretem Graecam damnas, atque Hellada totam,

The evil people, stir up their voices, while white
England holds true to its name of white
And triumphs in it.

15. *On the biretta*

Those dictums which the loud
Home-grown English enemy
Of the surplice pitches down,
The nearby hat
Hears, and seeks the very top
Of the head. Not so does even one
Corner escape the notice
Of acid words. Indeed now,
If you consider it,
For you and those
With you, the hat is far
Better than the wig, in that the brain's
Fever, which eats its way deep
Into your marrow, is cooled by it.
But you who are
So set against
Hats, which the Church has said
It approves, take care lest, in the end,
You attack its reverend Head.

16. *Against the Puritan*

Why do you think the Latin tongue to be
Sacrilegious, which older times
And our own times approve? Why do you

Quâ tamen occisi foedera scripta Dei?
Scilicet Hebraeam cantas, & perstrepis vnam: 5
    Haec facit ad nasum sola loquela tuum.

XVII. De Episcopis

Quos charos habuit Christus Apostolos,
Testatósque suo tradiderat gregi;
Vt, cùm mors rabidis vnguibus imminens
Doctrinae fluuios clauderet aureae,
Mites acciperent Lampada Praesules,   5
Seruaréntque sacrum clauibus ordinem;
Hos nunc barbaries impia vellicat
Indulgens proprijs ambitionibus,
Et, quos ipsa nequit scandere vertices,
Hos ad se trahere et mergere gestiens.   10
O caecum populum! si bona res siet
Praesul, cur renuis? sin mala, pauculos
Quàm cunctos fieri praestat Episcopos.

XVIII. Ad Melvinum de ijsdem

Praesulibus dirum te Musa coarguit hostem,
    An quia Textores Artificésque probas?

Damn all Hellas, sculptured Greek,
Even though the slain God's covenants
Were written in it? No doubt you sing
In Hebrew only, and make a racket:
This language only suits your nose.

17. *On the bishops*

Those Apostles Christ held dear,
And gave them to his flock
When they had testified to him,
So that when death, hanging over
With hungry nails, should shut the brooks
Of doctrine's gold, mild bishops might
Receive the torches, and with their keys
Keep the holy lineage intact—
Rude evil, sunk in its own ambitions,
Taunts them now, and since it can't
Go up those heights itself, rejoices
To pull them down and sink them to its level.
O blind people! If the bishop
Is a good thing, why do you deny it?
If evil, better to have of bishops
Very few, than everyone a bishop.

18. *To Melville: on the same*

Does the Muse clearly prove you to be the bishops'
    implacable foe,
Or is it because to weavers and craftsmen you never say
    no?

XIX. De Textore Catharo

Cum piscatores Textor legit esse vocatos,
   Vt sanctum Domini persequerentur opus;
Ille quoque inuadit Diuinam Flaminis artem,
   Subtegmen reti dignius esse putans,
Et nunc perlongas Scripturae stamine telas   5
   Torquet, & in Textu Doctor vtroque cluet.

XX. De Magicis rotatibus

Quos tu rotatus, quale murmur auscultas
In ritibus nostris? Ego audio nullum.
Agè, prouocemus vsque ad Angelos ipsos,
Aurésque superas: arbitri ipsi sint litis,
Vtrum tenore sacra nostra sint nécne   5
Aequabili facta. Ecquid ergo te tanta
Calumniandi concitauit vrtica,
Vt, quae Papicolis propria, assuas nobis,
Falsúmque potiùs quàm crepes [verum] versu?
Tu perstrepis tamen; vtque turgeat carmen   10
Tuum tibi, poeta belle, non mystes,
Magicos rotatus, & perhorridas Striges,
Dicterijs mordacibus notans, clamas
Non conuenire precibus ista Diuinis.
O saeuus hostis! quàm ferociter pugnas!   15
Nihílne respondebimus tibi? Fatemur.

19. *On the Puritan weaver*

When the weaver reads that fishermen
Were called to fructify the holy work
Of the Lord, he too invades
The priesthood's godly skill, thinking
The woof better than the net; and now
He twists endless threads throughout
The warp of Scripture, and in
Both weaves is famed a learned man.

20. *On magic dervishing*

What dervishing, what kind of
Murmur do you overhear
In our rites? I hear nothing.
Come now, we must plead
To the very angels, and heaven's ears:
Let them be the judges of the argument
—Whether our sacred rites have been performed
In a steady course or not.
Has so keen a thorn of slander
Pierced you, that those things
Which belong to Papists only
You stick on us, and stress,
Rather than the true, the untrue
In your verse? And still
You bang about; and that your song,
Sweet one (not priest but poet), may swell,
You, with acid comments, shout
That magic dervishing, horrid screech owls,

XXI. *Ad fratres*

O Sec'lum lepidum! circumstant vndique Fratres,
    Papicolísque sui sunt, Catharísque sui.
Sic nunc plena boni sunt omnia Fratris, amore
    Cùm nil fraterno rarius esse queat.

XXII. *De labe maculísque*

Labeculas maculásque nobis obijcis:
Quid? hoccine est mirum? Viatores sumus.
Quò sanguis est Christi, nisi vt maculas lauet,
Quas spargit animae corporis propius lutum?
Vos ergo puri! o nomen appositissimum   5
Quo vulgus ornat vos! At audias parum;
Astronomus olim (vt fama) dum maculas diu,
Quas Luna habet, tuetur, in foueam cadit,
Totúsque caenum Cynthiae ignoscit notis.
Ecclesia est mihi Luna; perge in Fabulâ.   10

Do not belong with excellence of prayer.
O hard enemy! How ferociously you fight!
Will we say nothing back to you?
We will not.

21. *To the brotherhood*

O gracious age! On every side
The brothers stand around.
Puritans and Papists have
Each their own. So now there are
Good brothers everywhere, though nothing
Can be rarer than a brother's love.

22. *On spots and stains*

You reproach us for
Imperfections, stains.
Why? Is it so
Strange? We are
Travelers. What
Is Christ's blood for, save
To wash stains off,
Which the body's clay, too intimate,
Sprinkles on the spirit?
You are therefore pure!
Oh, the name the crowd
Puts on you is most
Fitting. But listen

XXIII. De Musicâ Sacrâ

Cur efficaci, Deucalion, manu,
Post restitutos fluctibus obices,
   Mutas in humanam figuram
      Saxa superuacuásque cautes?

Quin redde formas, o bone, pristinas,   5
Et nos reducas ad lapides auos:
   Nam saxa mirantur canentes,
      Saxa lyras citharásque callent.

Rupes tenaces & silices ferunt
Potentiori carmine percitas   10
   Saltus per incultos lacúsque
      Orphea mellifluum secutas.

Et saxa diris hispida montibus
Amphionis testudine nobili

Just a little:
Once upon a time
(As they tell) an astronomer,
As he was long observing
The spots the moon had, fell
In a ditch, and totally
Forgot the filth in
The stains of Cynthia.
To me the moon
Is the Church:
Take it from there!

23. On sacred music [3]

Why, Deucalion, by the craft of your hand,
After barriers were set to the waves again,
Did you change the stones and useless
Rocks into human shapes?

Indeed, good man, restore the first forms,
Bring us back to stone, our ancestor,
For stones admire singers, stones
Understand the lyre and the cithara.

They say irascible cliffs, rocks, were roused
By song more powerful than they,
And followed through wilderness and lake
The honey-liquid song of Orpheus.

And jagged rocks on frightening mountains
By Amphion's noble lyre stunned,

Percussa dum currunt ad vrbem 15
    Moenia contribuêre Thebis.

Tantùm repertum est trux hominum genus,
Qui templa sacris expoliant choris,
    Non erubescentes vel ipsas
        Duritiâ superare cautes. 20

O plena centum Musica Gratijs,
Praeclariorum spirituum cibus,
    Quò me vocas tandem, tuúmque
        Vt celebrem decus insusurras?

Tu Diua miro pollice spiritum 25
Caeno profani corporis exuens
    Ter millies coelo reponis:
        Astra rogant, Nouus hic quis hospes?

Ardore Moses concitus entheo,
Mersis reuertens laetus ab hostibus 30
    Exuscitat plebem sacratos
        Ad Dominum properare cantus.

Quid hocce? Psalmos audión? o dapes!
O succulenti balsama spiritûs!
    Ramenta coeli, guttulaéque 35
        Deciduae melioris orbis!

Quos David, ipsae deliciae Dei,
Ingens piorum gloria Principum,
    Sionis excelsas ad arces
        Cum citharis lituísque miscet. 40

As they tumbled down to the city,
Imparted city walls to Thebes.

Only the race of man has been discovered savage,
Who decks his temples out with sacred choirs,
And yet is not ashamed to be in hardness
Harder than the stones themselves.

O music, filled with a hundred charms,
Food of spirits more glorified,
Whither do you summon me, I pray,
And whisper me to say abroad your beauty?

You, Goddess, with an amazing thumb releasing
The spirit from the filth of an unholy body,
Return it to the sky three thousandfold:
"Who is this new guest?" the stars inquire.

Moses, excited with a God-inspired passion,
Returning joyous from the drowning
Of the enemy, stirred the people up to hurry
A holy music to the Lord.

What is this? Don't I hear Psalms?
O holy banquets! O soothing
Oil of the spirit! Flakes of heaven, falling
Droplets of a better world!

David, himself the favorite of God,
The high excellence of holy kings,
In Sion's lofty places mingles those
Psalms with the trumpet and the cithara.

Miratur aequor finitimum sonos,
Et ipse Iordan sistit aquas stupens;
    Prae quo Tibris vultum recondit,
        Eridanúsque pudore fusus.

Tún obdis aures, grex noue, barbaras,   45
Et nullus audis? cantibus obstrepens,
    Vt, quò fatiges verberésque
        Pulpita, plus spatij lucreris?

At cui videri prodigium potest
Mentes, quietis tympana publicae,   50
    Discordijs plenas sonoris
        Harmoniam tolerare nullam?

XXIV. De eâdem

Cantus sacros, profane, mugitus vocas?
    Mugire multò mauelim quàm rudere.

XXV. De rituum vsu

Cum primùm ratibus suis
nostram Caesar ad insulam
olim appelleret, intuens
omnes indigenas loci
viuentes sine vestibus,   5
O victoria, clamitat,
certa, ac perfacilis mihi!

The near sea wonders at the noise,
And the Jordan itself, astonished, checks
Its waters; compared with it the Tiber hides
Its face, as does the Po, put to shame.

O new flock, do you shut your rude ears
And fail to hear, noisy in opposition to the songs,
That you may get a better chance
To beat and wear your pulpits out?

But to whom can it appear a wonder
That minds that are the timbrels of the common peace,
Minds filled up with ringing discords,
Can tolerate no harmony?

24. *On the same*

Sacred songs are lowing, you say?
Blasphemer, I'd rather low than bray.

25. *On the use of rites*

Long ago, when Caesar
First set foot from his ships
Upon our isle,
Noting all the natives of the place
Living without clothes, he cried,
"O victory is mine!
It will be simple,
It is assured!"

Non alio Cathari modo
dum sponsam Domini pijs
orbam ritibus expetunt, 10
atque ad barbariem patrum
vellent omnia regredi,
illam tegminis insciam
prorsus Daemoni & hostibus
exponunt superabilem. 15
   Atqui vos secus, o boni,
sentire ac sapere addecet,
si vestros animos regant
Scripturae canones sacrae:
Namque haec, iure, cuipiam 20
vestem non adimi suam,
sed nudis & egentibus
non suam tribui iubet.

XXVI. *De annulo coniugali*

Sed nec coniugij signum, Melvine, probabis?
   Nec vel tantillum pignus habebit amor?
Nulla tibi si signa placent, è nubibus arcum
   Eripe coelesti qui moderatur aquae.
Illa quidem à nostro non multùm abludit imago, 5
   Annulus & plenus tempore forsan erit.
Sin nebulis parcas, & nostro parcito signo,

And so the Puritans,
While they are covetous of a
Lord's bride bare of sacred rites,
And while they wish
All things regressed
To their fathers' barbaric state,
Lay her, entirely
Ignorant of clothing, bare to conquest
By Satan and her enemies.

O good men,
It becomes you to think
Another way, to be wise,
If Scripture's sacred canons
Govern you: for these
Do not tell a man to be
Robbed of clothes belonging to him,
But rather bid that clothes
They do not own themselves
Be given to the poor.

26. *On the wedding ring*

But won't you even, Melville,
Assent to the sign of marriage?
Will love not even have so small
A pledge? If no sign pleases you,
Rip from the clouds the rainbow
Which moderates the waters of heaven.
Indeed, that image is not much
Unlike our own, and in time, perhaps, its circle

Cui non absimilis sensus inesse solet.
Scilicet, vt quos ante suas cum coniuge tedas
   Merserat in lustris perniciosa venus,   10
Annulus hos reuocet, sistátque libidinis vndas
   Legitimi signum connubiale tori.

XXVII. *De Mundis et mundanis*

Ex praelio vndae ignísque (si Physicis fides)
   Tranquillus aer nascitur:
Sic ex profano Cosmico & Catharo potest
   Christianus extundi bonus.

XXVIII. *De oratione Dominicâ*

Quam Christus immortalis innocuo gregi
   voce suâ dederat,
         quis crederet mortalibus
orationem reijci septemplicem,
   quae miseris clypeo   5
         Aiacis est praestantior?
Haec verba superos aduolaturus thronos

Will be completed. If you spare clouds,
Be lenient with our sign as well,
In which there often is a sense
Not unlike this, which is that those
Whom lust dipped in lewd deeds
Before they joined their mates in marriage
The ring retrieves, and that the sign
Of marriage's true bond the waters
Of unbridled desire stills.

27. On the worldly and the unworldly

From battle of water and fire
(If you believe the doctors)
The tranquil air is shaped:
So from unholy worldling
And the Puritan, a good
Christian can be hammered out.

28. On the Lord's Prayer

Who would have thought
The prayer in seven parts which Christ,
Who has no death in him,
Gave to the naive flock in his own voice,
To be cast out by mortal men,
And which, to the wretched, is better
Than the shield of Ajax? Christ,
About to take wing to Paradise,

Christus, vt auxilij
        nos haud inanes linqueret,
(cùm dignius nil posset aut melius dare)   10
    pignora chara sui
        fruenda nobis tradidit.
Quis sic amicum excipiet, vt Cathari Deum,
    qui renouare sacri
        audent amoris Symbolum?   15
Tu verò quisquis es, caue ne, dum neges,
    improbe, verba Dei,
        te deneget VERBVM Deus.

XXIX. *In Catharum quendam*

Cum templis effare, madent sudaria, mappae,
    Trux caper alarum, suppara, laena, sagum.
Quin populo, clemens, aliquid largire caloris:
    Nunc sudas solus; caetera turba riget.

Delivered us (since he could have given
Nothing more right or sweet) these words as
Dear pledges of himself for us to relish,
That he might not deny us,
The empty-handed ones, any
Help at all. Who will receive
A friend the way the Puritans, who dare
Touch up anew the symbol
Of holy love, do their God?
But you, whoever you may be, take care,
Lest, evil one, while you deny
The words of God, God's Word
Abandon you.

29. *On a certain Puritan*

When in churches
You emote,
Handkerchiefs, napkins,
Armpits,
Linen shirts,
Lined cloaks, woolen
Cloaks get wet. Sweet fellow,
Why not lavish on the people
Some heat? Now you alone
Sweat; the rest
Of the mob is cold.

XXX. De lupâ lustri Vaticani

Calumniarum nec pudor quis nec modus?
Nec *Vaticanae* desines vnquam *Lupae*
Metus inanes? Nos pari praeteruehi
Illam Charybdim cautione nouimus
Vestrámque Scyllam, aequis parati spiculis   5
Britannicam in Vulpem, ínque Romanam Lupam.
Dicti fidem firmabimus Anagrammate.

XXXI. De impositione manuum

Nec dextra te fugit, almi Amoris emblema?
Atqui manus imponere integras praestat,
Quàm (more vestro) imponere inscio vulgo.
Quantò Impositio melior est Imposturâ!

30. *On the she-wolf of the Vatican brothel*

Is there no shame
Or end of slander?
Will you never cast aside
Your vain fears of the Vatican
She-wolf? We know,
With equal care, to pass by
That Charybdis and your Scylla,
Prepared with impartial spears
Against the British fox
And the Roman she-wolf.
In an anagram[4] I shall assert
My confidence in what I've said.

31. *About the laying on of hands*

Does not the right hand even,
The emblem of healing love,
Escape you? Indeed, it is better
To lay on pure hands,
Than, by your custom,
To impose upon the ignorant crowd.
How much better than imposture is
The imposition of hands.

XXXII. *Supplicum Ministrorum raptus* κωμῳδούμενος

    Ambitio Cathari quinque constat Actibus.
 I. Primò, vnus aut alter parum ritus placet:
    Iam repit impietas volatura illico.
 II. Mox displicent omnes. Vbi hoc permanserit
III. Paulò, secretis mussitans in angulis   5
    Quaerit recessus. Incalescit fabula:
 IV. Erumpit inde, & contineri nescius
  V. Syluas pererrat. Fibulis dein omnibus
    Prae spiritu ruptis, quò eas resarciat
    Amstellodamum corripit se. *Plaudite.*   10

XXXIII. *De Autorum enumeratione*

Quò magìs inuidiam nobis & crimina confles,
    Pertrahis in partes nomina magna tuas;
Martyra, Calvinum, Bezam, doctúmque *Bucerum,*
    Qui tamen in nostros fortiter ire negant.
Whitaker, erranti quem praefers carmine, miles   5
    Assiduus nostri papilionis erat.
Nos quoque possemus longas conscribere turmas,
    Si numero starent praelia, non animis.
Primus adest nobis, Pharisaeis omnibus hostis,
    Christus Apostolici cinctus amore gregis.   10
Tu geminas belli portas, o *Petre,* repandis,

32. *The frenzy of the petitioning ministers:*[5] *in the comic mode*

The Puritan's ambition is composed
Of five acts. First, one or the other rite
Displeases him. Now, soon about
To soar up, sacrilege crawls along.
Next, all rites irritate him.
When this persists a little, he, muttering
In secret corners, tries to get away.
The play warms up: he then
Breaks out, and beyond control,
Wanders in the woods. Then, with all the buttons
Upon the spirit popped, he rushes off
To Amsterdam to patch them up. (Applaud!)

33. *Concerning the enumeration of authors*

To instigate adverse opinions and incriminations
Against us, you highhandedly incorporate
Famous names to your side: Martyr, Calvin,
Beza, learned Bucer. But still they won't go
Against our cause. The Whitaker you praise
In heretical song, was a loyal warrior for us.
We too could make a long catalogue of forces
If battles hinged on numbers, not on spirits.
First on our side is Christ, a foe
To every Pharisee, and fenced about by love
Of the Apostolic flock. You, O Peter, open up
The gates of war, while Paul, taking out

Dum gladium stringens *Paulus* ad arma vocat.
Inde Patres pergunt quadrati, & tota Vetustas.
    Nempe Nouatores quis Veteranus amat?
Iam *Constantinus* multo se milite miscet;   15
    Inuisámque tuis erigit hasta Crucem.
Hipponensis adest properans, & torquet in hostes
    Lampada, quâ studijs inuigilare solet.
Téque Deum alternis cantans *Ambrosius* iram,
    Immemor antiqui mellis, eundo coquit.   20
Haec etiam ad pugnam praesens, quâ viuimus, aetas
    Innumeram nostris partibus addit opem.
Quos inter plenúsque Deo genióque Iacobus
    Defendit veram mente manúque *fidem.*
Interea ad sacrum stimulat sacra Musica bellum,   25
    Quâ sine vos miseri lentiùs itis ope.
Militat & nobis, quem vos contemnitis, Ordo;
    Ordine discerni maxima bella solent.
O vos inualidos! Audi quem talibus armis
    Euentum Naso vidit et admonuit;   30
Vna dies Catharos ad bellum miserat omnes:
    Ad bellum missos perdidit vna dies.

XXXIV. *De auri sacrâ fame*

Claudis auaritiâ Satyram; statuísque sacrorum
    Esse recidendas, Aeace noster, opes.

His sword, makes the call to arms. From there
The Fathers come, and all the early Church,
Arranged in battle form. What old warrior,
Indeed, loves an innovator? With many soldiers
Constantine comes over to us, and raises up
The cross your men despise. Augustine,
Hurrying, is here, and pitches at the foe
The torch he's used to tend his studies
Minutely by; and Ambrose, forgetting classic sweetness,
Intoning *Te Deum's* antiphons, simmers
His anger as he goes.
This age in which we live, advancing also
To the fight, adds a numberless force to our side.
Among them James, full of genius and God,
Guards the true faith with mind and body.
Meanwhile sacred music excites to sacred battle,
A help without which you unfortunate people
Go forward at a slower rate. The Order[6] you look down
    on
Also fights for us, and order as a rule
Is the deciding factor in the greatest battles.
O feeble ones! Hear the end of such array,
That Ovid saw and brought back to your minds:
"It took one day to send all the Puritans[7] to war;
Once sent, it took one day to wipe them out."

34. On the infernal greed for gold

On greed you close your satire,
For you decide, our Aeacus, elaboration

Caetera condonabo tibi, scombrísque remittam:
Sacrilegum carmen, censeo, flamma voret.

XXXV. *Ad Scotiam. Protrepticon ad Pacem*

Scotia quae frigente iaces porrecta sub Arcto,
    Cur adeò immodicâ relligione cales?
Anne tuas flammas ipsa Antiperistasis auget,
    Vt niue torpentes incaluêre manus?
Aut vt pruna gelu summo mordaciùs vrit,   5
    Sic acuunt zelum frigora tanta tuum?
Quin nocuas extingue faces, precor: vnda propinqua est,
    Et tibi vicinas porrigit aequor aquas:
Aut potiùs Christi sanguis demissus ab alto,
    Vicinúsque magìs nobiliórque fluit: 10
Ne, si flamma nouis adolescat mota flabellis,
    Ante diem vestro mundus ab igne ruat.

Must be cut away from rites.
All your other written things
I will deliver up to you;
To mackerel I will return them:
I think the flames should eat
Your sacrilegious song.

35. *To Scotland: an exhortation to peace*

Scotland, lying
Stretched out under Arctic cold,
Why do you burn up so much
In a radical religion?
Does the sudden change itself
Add to your flames,
As hands, benumbed by snow
Grow warm? Or, as the ember burns
Keener in a deeper cold,
Does so much frost thus stimulate
Your zeal? Rather, I pray you,
Put out the perilous torches:
The water is near, for you its surface
Extends the neighbor sea;
Or rather Christ's blood dispatched
From above, a closer and a nobler thing,
Flows forth. Put out the torches,
Lest, if your flames fanned anew leap up,
The world before the day appointed
Collapse from your fire.

XXXVI. *Ad seductos innocentes*

Innocuae mentes, quibus inter flumina mundi
   Ducitur illimi candida vita fide,
Absit vt ingenuum pungant mea verba pudorem;
   Perstringunt vestros carmina sola duces.
O vtinam aut illorum oculi (quod comprecor vnum)   5
   Vobis, aut illis pectora vestra forent.

XXXVII. *Ad Melvinum*

Atqui te precor vnicè per ipsam,
Quae scripsit numeros, manum; per omnes
Musarum calices, per & beatos
Sarcasmos quibus artifex triumphas;
Quin per Presbyteros tuos; per vrbem   5
Quam curto nequeo referre versu;
Per charas tibi nobilésque dextras,
Quas subscriptio neutiquam inquinauit;
Per quicquid tibi suauiter probatur;
Ne me carminibus nimis dicacem,   10
Aut saeuum reputes. Amica nostra est
Atque edentula Musa, nec veneno
Splenis perlita contumeliosi.
   Nam si te cuperem secare versu,

36. *To the innocent who have been seduced*

Childlike minds, who
Among the muddy waters of the world
A white life lead
In clear faith, God forbid
That my words hurt
Your meek honesty.
Your leaders only
Do these songs touch upon.
This one prayer I make:
Oh, if only you possessed their eyes,
Or they your hearts!

37. *To Melville*

But in particular by that hand which wrote the poems,
I pray; by all the wine cups
Of the Muses, and by the blessed wit
By which you triumph as an artist; indeed,
By your presbyters; by the city[8] which
I can't record in a short verse;
By the noble right hands dear to you which
In no way did a signature[9] debase;
By whatever is by you approved in sweetness:
You must not think me cruel or over-witty
In singing. For nice, for toothless is my Muse,
Not sweating with the poison of a vulgar spleen.
    If I desired to hurt you in a verse,
And all my anger vomited in force
Which the Church your friends despised,

Totámque euomerem potenter iram   ¹⁵
Quam aut Ecclesia despicata vobis,
Aut laesae mihi suggerunt Athenae,
(Et quem non stimularet haec simultas?)
Iam te funditus igneis Camoenis,
Et Musâ crepitante subruissem: ²⁰
Omnis linea sepiam recusans
Plumbo ducta fuisset aestuanti,
Centum stigmatibus tuos inurens
Profanos fremitus bonásque sannas:
Plùs charta haec mea delibuta dictis   ²⁵
Haesisset tibi, quàm suprema vestis
Olim accreuerit *Herculi* furenti:
Quin hoc carmine Lexicon probrorum
Extruxissem, vbi, cùm moneret vsus,
Haurirent tibi tota plaustra Musae.   ³⁰
    Nunc haec omnia sustuli, tonantes
Affectus socijs tuis remittens.
Non te carmine turbidum vocaui,
Non deridiculúmue, siue ineptum,
Non striges, magiámue, vel rotatus,   ³⁵
Non fastus tibi turgidos repono;
Errores, maculas, superbiámque,
Labes, somniáque, ambitúsque diros,
Tinnitus *Berecynthios* omittens
Nil horum regero tibi merenti.   ⁴⁰
    Quin te laudibus orno: quippe dico,
Caesar sobrius ad rei Latinae
Vnus dicitur aduenire cladem:
Et tu solus ad *Angliae* procellas
(Cùm plerumque tuâ sodalitate   ⁴⁵

Or Athens having been abused, stores up in me
(And who would not be stirred up by this quarrel?),
I would by now, with fiery Latin Muses,
And with a crackling Greek one, have utterly destroyed
    you:
Every line, avoiding ink,
Searing with a hundred scars
Your ungodly noises and your goodly frowns,
Would have been drawn in flaming lead:
This my paper, smeared with words,
Would have stuck to you more
Than once adhered to raving Hercules
The last cloak he wore. So by this song
I should have built abuse's lexicon
Where the Muses might, as use so counseled,
Tap whole barrelfuls for you.
    Now I have refrained from all of these,
Leaving for your friends bombast's beloved things.
In song I have not called you mad,
Not ridiculous or silly, nor reimbursed you
With screech owls or enchantresses or twirlers,
And not with puffed up airs;
Stains, insolence, heresies,
Ruins, dreams, and dire ambiguities—
I, excluding Berecynthian
Cymbal-tinkling,[10] have pitched back none of these on
    you,
Though you deserve it. With praises rather
I gild you: for I say it's well known that
Caesar was the only sober man
Who went about the ruin of the Latin state;
And it is you who stir up on your own
(Though there is nothing than your sect in general

Nil sit crassius, impolitiúsue)
Accedis bene doctus, et poeta.

XXXVIII. Ad Eundem

Incipis irridens; stomachans in carmine pergis;
   Desinis exclamans: tota figura, vale.

XXXIX. Ad Seren. Regem

Ecce pererratas, Regum doctissime, nugas,
Quas gens inconsulta, suis vexata procellis,
Libandas nobis absorbendásque propinat!
O caecos animi fratres! quis vestra fatigat
Corda furor, spissáque afflat caligine sensus?   5
Cernite, quàm formosa suas Ecclesia pennas
Explicat, & radijs ipsum pertingit Olympum!
Vicini populi passim mirantur, & aequos
Mentibus attonitis cupiunt addiscere ritus:
Angelicae turmae nostris se coetibus addunt: 10
Ipse etiam Christus coelo speculatus ab alto,
Intuitúque vno stringens habitacula mundi,
Sola mihi plenos, ait, exhibet *Anglia* cultus.
Scilicet has olim diuisas aequore terras
Seposuit Diuina sibi, cùm conderet orbem,   15
Progenies, gemmámque suâ quasi pyxide clausit.
    O qui *Defensor Fidei* meritissimus audis,
Responde aeternùm titulo; quóque ordine felix

More inelegant or crass)
English tempests, a poet and a learned man.

38. *To the same*

Jeering you begin, jumpy you keep on
In poetry, yelling you quit: farewell, cartoon.

39. *To His Serene Majesty*

Most learned king, see the commonplaces which a silly
    brood,
Shaken by its own dissensions, gives us to taste
And take as drink! O brothers, blind in spirit,
What insanity fatigues your hearts, and blows
Upon your senses in a thick vapor? See how
The lovely Church outspreads its wings and sheds
Its radiance as far as heaven. Far and wide
The neighbor nations wonder, and, their minds adazzle,
Want to learn a ritual in harmony with yours.
Angelic hosts increase our company;
And Christ himself, watching from the skies,
Taking in the houses of the world at a glance,
Says that only England offers him a finished worship.
Sure when he shaped the world, the Seed of God
Set aside for him these sea-divided lands of old,
And shut them like a jewel in his jewel box.
You, most rightly called Defender of the Faith,
Forever answer to your title, and in the same

Coepisti, pergas simili res texere filo.
Obrue feruentes, ruptis conatibus, hostes: 20
Quásque habet aut patulas, aut caeco tramite, moles
Haeresis, euertas. Quid enim te fallere possit?
Tu venas laticésque omnes, quos sacra recludit
Pagina, gustâsti, multóque interprete gaudes:
Tu Synodósque, Patrésque, & quod dedit alta vetustas   25
Haud per te moritura, Scholámque introspicis omnem.
Nec transire licet quo mentis acumine findis
Viscera naturae, commistúsque omnibus astris
Ante tuum tempus coelum gratissimus ambis.
Hâc ope munitus securior excipis vndas,   30
Quas Latij Catharíque mouent, atque inter vtrasque
Pastor agis proprios, medio tutissimus, agnos.
    Perge, decus Regum; sic, Augustissime, plures
Sint tibi vel stellis laudes, & laudibus anni:
Sic pulsare tuas, exclusis luctibus, ausint   35
Gaudia sola fores: sic quicquid somnia mentis
Intus agunt, habeat certum meditatio finem:
Sic positis nugis, quibus irretita libido
Innumeros mergit vitiatâ mente poetas,
Sola *Iacobaeum* decantent carmina nomen.   40

Propitious way that you've begun, continue
In the same way to handle things. Overcome
The angry foe, having nipped his efforts; reverse
The might that heresy keeps out in the open
Or in a dark path. For what can fool you?
All the veins and liquids Holy Writ reveals
You've tasted, and joy in many commentators.
You examine Synods, the Fathers, and what
Deep antiquity, not meant to die through you,
Yields up, and the entire School. Nor can we
Overlook the mental brilliance by which
You part the hidden essences of Nature.
Mingled with all the stars, before your time,
Most well received, you make a try for heaven.
Endowed with this ability, you endure
With greater confidence as Puritans
And Roman Catholics arouse the waves
Between which you, the Shepherd, drive your sheep,
Safest in a *via media*.
   Keep on, ornament of kings.
Thus, your Excellence, may your praises
Outnumber stars, and your years your praises.
Thus, lamentations barred, may only
Joys dare beat upon your doors.
Thus, whatever mental fancies do within you,
May meditation have a fixed aim.
Thus, trifles put aside, which, entangling passion,
Force it to level innumerable poets in madness,
May melodies celebrate over and over
Nothing but the name of James.

XL. *Ad Deum*

Quem tu, summe Deus, semel
Scribentem placido rore beaueris,
   Illum non labor irritus
Exercet miserum; non dolor vnguium
   Morsus increpat anxios;   5
Non maeret calamus; non queritur caput:
   Sed faecunda poëseωs
Vis, & vena sacris regnat in artubus;
   Qualis nescius aggerum
Exundat fluuio Nilus amabili.   10
   O dulcissime Spiritus,
Sanctos qui gemitus mentibus inseris
   A Te Turture defluos,
Quòd scribo, & placeo, si placeo, tuum est.

40. *To God*

Once you, great God, bless
With sweet dew him who writes,
No futile labor makes it
A painful time for him; no aching
Fingers bother him for being bitten; no head
Aches, no quill is sad:
But in the pure body verse's
Ripe élan and vein are master,
Even as the Nile, unaware
Of dikes, overflows,
Lovely in its flooding. O sweetest
Spirit, you who fill up minds
With holy groans pouring
From you, the Dove, the writing
That I do, the pleasure that I give,
If I give it, is all from you.

Passio Discerpta

I. Ad Dominum morientem

Cum lacrymas oculósque duos tot vulnera vincant,
    Impar, & in fletum vel resolutus, ero;
Sepia concurrat, peccatis aptior humor,
    Et mea iam lacrymet culpa colore suo.

II. In sudorem sanguineum

Quò fugies, sudor? quamuìs pars altera Christi
    Nescia sit metae; venula, cella tua est.
Si tibi non illud placeat mirabile corpus,
    Caetera displiceat turba, necesse, tibi:
Ni me fortè petas; nam quantò indignior ipse,
    Tu mihi subueniens dignior esse potes.

5

The Events of the Passion[1]

1. *To the dying Lord*

Since so much wounding overcomes my eyes, my tears,
I will have no effect, though melted down in weeping.
Let ink help me out,
A liquid more akin to guilt;
Let my sins, now tinted right, pour forth their tears.

2. *On the bloody sweat*

Sweat, where will you go? No matter
How much the other side of Christ[2]
May know no limit, the vein
Is where you live. If that wondrous
Body does not please you, it follows
Neither would the crowd besides:
Unless perhaps you seek me; for the more
I am unworthy, the worthier
You can be, coming to help me.

III. In eundem

Sic tuus effundi gestit pro crimine sanguis,
   Vt nequeat paulò se cohibere domi.

IV. In latus perfossum

Christe, vbi tam duro patet in te semita ferro,
   Spero meo cordi posse patere viam.

V. In Sputum et Conuicia

O Barbaros! sic os rependitis sanctum,
Visum quod vni praebet, omnibus vitam,
Sputando, praedicando? sic Aquas vitae
Contaminatis alueósque caelestes
Sputando, blasphemando? nempe ne hoc fiat
In posterum, maledicta Ficus arescens
Gens tota fiet, atque vtrinque plectetur.
Parate situlas, Ethnici, lagenásque,
Graues lagenas, Vester est Aquae-ductus.

5

VI. In Coronam spineam

Christe, dolor tibi supplicio, mihi blanda voluptas;
   Tu spinâ miserè pungeris, ipse Rosâ.

3. On the same

Your blood joys to be poured out for sin so much,
It can't keep a drop of it at home.

4. On the pierced side

Christ, when remorseless steel has opened up a path in
      you,
I hope there can be opened up a pathway for my heart.

5. On the spitting and mocking

O barbaric men! Is this how you pay back the holy face,
Which gives sight to one, and life to all,
With spit, with oaths? Is this how you defile,
With spit and blasphemy, the waters
Of life and the sacred conduits?
So this won't come about again,
The whole nation will become
The fig tree under malediction, withering,
By God and pagan hounded! O Gentiles,
Fetch you jars and buckets—big jars to your well!

6. On the crown of thorns

Christ, your punishment is pain,
Mine delicious ease; you are pricked with thorns,

Spicula mutemus: capias Tu serta Rosarum,
Qui Caput es, spinas & tua Membra tuas.

VII. *In Arund. Spin. Genuflex. Purpur.*

Quàm nihil illudis, Gens improba! quàm malè cedunt
   Scommata! Pastorem semper Arundo decet.
Quàm nihil illudis! cùm quò magìs angar acuto
   Munere, Rex tantò verior inde prober.
Quàm nihil illudis flectens! namque integra posthâc   5
   Posteritas flectet córque genúque mihi.
Quàm nihil illudis! si, quae tua purpura fingit,
   Purpureo meliùs sanguine Regna probem.
At non lusus erit, si quem tu laeta necasti
   Viuat, & in mortem vita sit illa tuam.   10

VIII. *In Alapas*

Ah! quàm caederis hinc & inde palmis!
   Sic vnguenta solent manu fricari:
Sic toti medicaris ipse mundo.

I with the rose. Let us trade our hurts:
You, who are the head, take the rose for wreath,
And we, your members, take up your thorns.

7. On the reed, thorns, bowing down, and scarlet

How vain your fun, you wicked brood!
How badly jokes turn out!
How vain your fun! The reed
Will always be the shepherd's.
The more acute the gift of pain,
The truer King it proves I am.
How vain your fun, genuflecting!
For a pure people coming after this
Will bend their hearts and knees to me.
How vain your fun, if by my royal blood
I better demonstrate those kingdoms
Your scarlet simulates.
But it won't be a game
If he whom you are glad to murder lives,
And that life turns out
To be your death.

8. On the slaps

Ah, how with hands
You are on each side slapped!
It's thus that ointments are

IX. *In Flagellum*

Christe, flagellati spes & victoria mundi,
    Crimina cùm turgent, & mea poena prope est,
Suauiter admoueas notum tibi carne flagellum,
    Sufficiat virgae saepiùs vmbra tuae.
Mitis agas: tenerae duplicant sibi verbera mentes,   5
    Ipsáque sunt ferulae mollia corda suae.

X. *In vestes diuisas*

Si, Christe, dum suffigeris, tuae vestes
    Sunt hostium legata, non amicorum,
Vt postulat mos; quid tuis dabis? Teipsum.

Wont to be rubbed in the hand:
It's thus you yourself
Make well all the world.

9. *On the whip*

Christ, hope and triumph
Of the whip-tormented world,
When accusations swell
And my punishment is near,
Make sweetly imminent the lash,
Which in the flesh you've known;
More often make the shadow
Of your staff suffice.
Be gentle: tender minds
Compound the blows upon them,
And meek hearts are whips
Unto themselves.

10. *On the portioned garments*

If, Christ, while you are nailed,
Your garments are inheritance
To enemies and not to friends
As custom rules, what
Will you give your friends?
You yourself.

XI. *In pium Latronem*

O nimium Latro! reliquis furatus abundè,
   Nunc etiam Christum callidus aggrederis.

XII. *In Christum crucem ascensurum*

Zacchaeus, vt Te cernat, arborem scandit:
Nunc ipse scandis, vt labore mutato
Nobis facilitas cedat & tibi sudor.
Sic omnibus videris ad modum visûs.
Fides gigantem sola, vel facit nanum.   5

XIII. *Christus in cruce*

Hic, vbi sanati stillant opobalsama mundi,
   Aduoluor madidae laetus hiánsque Cruci:
Pro lapsu stillarum abeunt peccata; nec acres
   Sanguinis insultus exanimata ferunt.
Christe, fluas semper; ne, si tua flumina cessent,   5
   Culpa redux iugem te neget esse Deum.

11. *On the good thief*

O too much a thief! You have stolen
A great deal from everyone
Else; now also, crafty, you go up to Christ.

12. *To Christ about to ascend the cross*

Zacchaeus, that he might see you,
Climbed a tree: now you yourself
Climb up, so that, the work turned round,
Ease may be stored up for us,
And sweat for you. And so to each you seem
According to his way of seeing: faith
Alone makes a giant or a dwarf.

13. *Christ on the cross*

Here, where the healed world's
Smooth balm distilled,
I, joyous, and my mouth wide open,
Am driven to the drenched cross:
By the falling of that distillation,
Sins depart; dead things, they cannot bear
That blood's rigorous assaults.
Christ, keep welling up, for if your flooding stops,
Revived guilt will say you're not eternal God.

XIV. In Clauos

Qualis eras, qui, ne melior natura minorem
    Eriperet nobis, in Cruce fixus eras;
Iam meus es: nunc Te teneo: Pastórque prehensus
    Hoc ligno, his clauis est, quasi Falce suâ.

XV. Inclinato capite, JOH. 19

Vulpibus antra feris, nidíque volucribus adsunt,
    Quodque suum nouit strôma, cubile suum.
Qui tamen excipiat, Christus caret hospite: tantùm
    In cruce suspendens, vnde reclinet, habet.

XVI. Ad Solem deficientem

Quid hoc? & ipse deficis, Caeli gigas,
    Almi choragus luminis?
Tu promis Orbem manè, condis vesperi,
    Mundi fidelis clauiger:
At nunc fatiscis. Nempe Dominus aedium
    Prodegit integrum penu,
Quámque ipse lucis tesseram sibi negat,
    Negat familiae suae.

5

14. On the nails

What a wondrous being you were, who,
Lest the God-nature rip away
The human from us, were pinned on the cross.
Now you are mine, I hold you now:
By this wood the Shepherd has been seized,
And by these nails—as by his own
Pruning hook.

15. On the bowed head

Caves belong to wild foxes, and nests to birds;
Each thing knows its nook. But Christ
Has no host to shelter him.
Hanging on the cross, he has only
A place in which to languish.

16. On the sun in eclipse

What's this? You too gone out,
Giant of heaven, master of light
That fructifies? You unwrap your circle
In the morning, and in the evening
You cover it, faithful porter
Of the world. But now you fail.
For sure the Master of the house
Has wasted everything
From his store; the ration of light

Carere discat verna, quo summus caret
 Paterfamilias lumine.
Tu verò mentem neutiquam despondeas,
 Resurget occumbens Herus:
Tunc instruetur lautiùs radijs penu,
 Tibi supererunt & mihi.

XVII. *Monumenta aperta*

Dum moreris, Mea Vita, ipsi vixere sepulti,
 Próque vno vincto turba soluta fuit.
Tu tamen, haud tibi tam moreris, quàm viuis in illis,
 Asserit & vitam Mors animata tuam.
Scilicet in tumulis Crucifixum quaerite, viuit: 5
 Conuincunt vnam multa sepulcra Crucem.
Sic, pro Maiestate, Deum, non perdere vitam
 Quam tribuit, verùm multiplicare decet.

He keeps back from himself he
Keeps back from his own.
Let the houseboy learn to go
Without light, even as the Master of the house
Goes without it. But do not
By any means lose heart: the Master
Of the house, dying, will arise:
Then with beams the store will be
(More lavish than before) filled up:
For you and me there will be
More than enough.

17. *The opened tombs*

As you died, my Life, the very dead
Beneath the ground woke up, and by
Virtue of a single prisoner
Many have been loosed. And yet
You do not so much die to you
As you live in others, and Death,
Having had the breath of life
Breathed into him, assumes your life.
Yes, seek the Crucified in tombs!
He lives! Many sepulchers
Negate this single cross. Thus it is right
For God, because he is a king,
Not to waste the life he gave,
But make it grow.

XVIII. Terrae-motus

Te fixo vel Terra mouet: nam, cum Cruce, totam
  Circumferre potes; Sampson vt antè fores.
Heu stolidi, primùm fugientem figite Terram,
  Tunc Dominus clauis aggrediendus erit.

XIX. Velum scissum

Frustra, Verpe, tumes, propola cultûs,
Et Templi parasite; namque velum
Diffissum reserat Deum latentem,
Et pomoeria terminósque sanctos
Non vrbem facit vnicam, sed Orbem.   5
Et pro pectoribus recenset aras,
Dum cor omne suum sibi requirat
Structorem, & Solomon vbique regnet.
Nunc Arcana patent, nec inuolutam
Phylacteria complicant latrîam.   10
Excessit tener Orbis ex Ephebis,
Maturúsque suos coquens amores
Praeflorat sibi nuptias futuras.
Vbique est Deus, Agnus, Ara, Flamen.

18. *The movement of the earth*

With you nailed up, even
The earth moves: for with the cross
You move the whole thing to and fro
As Sampson moved the pillars long ago.
O dull-witted men,
First pin down the running earth!
Then you can assail the Lord with nails.

19. *The ripped veil*

You, Jew,
Huckster of worship, sponger
Of the Temple, you strut in vain,
For the ripped veil
Discloses the hidden God,
And makes the outer walls, and the sacred
Inner Temple grounds themselves,
Not one city only, but a world.
Instead of looking into hearts
As hearts, he looks for altars there,
Till every heart shall seek its maker,
And Solomon shall govern everywhere.
Now mysteries are opened up;
Phylacteries do not hedge a covered
Worship in a maze. The youthful world
Has departed from its youth,
And making of its ripened love a vintage,
Tastes before its time the fruits of marriage.
And God is everywhere—
The Lamb, the Priest, the Altar too.

XX. *Petrae scissae*

Sanus Homo factus, vitiorum purus vterque;
    At sibi collisit fictile Daemon opus.
Post vbi Mosaicae repararent fragmina Leges,
    Infectas tabulas facta iuuenca scidit.
Haud aliter cùm Christus obit, prae funere tanto   5
    Constat inaccessas dissiluisse petras.
Omnia, praeter corda, scelus confregit & error,
    Quae contrita tamen caetera damna leuant.

XXI. *In Mundi sympathiam cum Christo*

Non moreris solus: Mundus simul interit in te,
    Agnoscítque tuam Machina tota Crucem.
Hunc ponas animam mundi, Plato: vel tua mundum
    Ne nimium vexet quaestio, pone meam.

20. The cleft rocks

Man was fashioned whole, Adam
And Eve unstained by vice.
But the Devil for his own
Sake broke the clay.
When in after times
The Mosaic covenant
Fixed the pieces,
A brazen heifer broke
And wrecked the tablets.
When Christ died, it was
The same: unscalable
Crags collapsed
Under so much death. Error
And sin have broken everything
Except the heart. Hearts,
However, when ground to powder lighten
All other losses.

21. On the harmony of the world with Christ

You do not die alone:
The world, at the same
Time, dies in you,
And the whole mechanism
Is with your cross in tune.
Plato, in this man find
The Spirit of the World;
Or, lest your inquiry
Distress the world too much,
Look for Him in me.

Lucus

I. Homo, Statua

Sum, quis nescit, Imago Dei, sed saxea certè:
    Hanc mihi duritiem contulit improbitas.
Durescunt proprijs euulsa corallia fundis,
    Haud secus ingenitis dotibus orbus Adam.
Tu, qui cuncta creans docuisti marmora flere,   5
    Haud mihi cor saxo durius esse sinas.

II. Patria

Ut tenuis flammae species caelum vsque minatur,
    Igniculos legans, manserit ipsa licet;

The Sacred Grove

1. Man the statue

I am, stupid, the
Image of God but
Surely rock. Impurity
Put this hardness
On me. Red corals,
Pulled out
Of their habitat
Harden. The same
With Adam, bereft
Of his proper heritage.
You who
Creating all things gave
Marble the power to weep,
Do not let my heart
Be harder than stone.

2. Homeland

As the form of rarefied flame
Shooting off sparks leaps to the sky, though it

Sic mucronatam reddunt suspiria mentem,
  Votáque scintillae sunt animosa meae.
Assiduo stimulo carnem Mens vlta lacessit,   5
  Sedula si fuerit, perterebrare potest.

III. *In Stephanum lapidatum*

Qui silicem tundit, (mirum tamen) elicit ignem:
  At Caelum è saxis elicuit Stephanus.

IV. *In Simonem Magum*

Ecquid emes Christum? pro nobis scilicet olim
  Venditus est Agnus, non tamen emptus erit.
Quin nos Ipse emit, precioso faenora soluens
  Sanguine: nec precium merx emit vlla suum.
Ecquid emes Caelum? quin stellam rectiùs vnam   5
  Quo precio venit, fac, liceare priùs.
Nempe graui fertur scelerata pecunia motu,
  Si sursum iacias, in caput ipsa ruit.
Vnicus est nummus, caelo Christóque petitus,
  Nempe in quo clarè lucet Imago Dei.   10

Stays back itself, so do sighs
Make sharp the mind, and fiery prayers
Are my sparks. In pain
The mind beats the body all the time—
And if it perseveres,
Can tunnel through it.

3. On the stoning of Stephen

How marvelous! Who
Pounds rock gets fire.
But Stephen from
Stones got heaven.

4. On Simon Magus

Will you buy Christ?
No doubt long ago
The Lamb was sold for us; yet he will
Not be bought. No,
He bought us, liquidating
Our debt with his
Rich blood. No goods
Can buy their price.
Will you buy heaven?
Rather, it's better first
Your bid for one star be
As high as what it costs.
Surely tainted money

V. In S. Scripturas

Heu, quis spiritus, igneúsque turbo
Regnat visceribus, meásque versat
Imo pectore cogitationes?
Nunquid pro foribus sedendo nuper
Stellam vespere suxerim volantem,　　　　　　　5
Haec autem hospitio latere turpi
Prorsùs nescia, cogitat recessum?
Nunquid mel comedens, apem comedi
Ipsâ cum dominâ domum vorando?
Imò, me nec apes, nec astra pungunt:　　　　　10
Sacratissima Charta, tu fuisti
Quae cordis latebras sinúsque caecos
Atque omnes peragrata es angiportus
Et flexus fugientis appetitûs.
Ah, quàm docta perambulare calles　　　　　　15
Maeandrósque plicásque, quàm perita es!
Quae vis condidit, ipsa nouit aedes.

Has a heavy weight:
If you heave it upward, it
Falls upon your head.
There's but one kind of coin
Looked for by Christ and heaven;
Truly the one in which
God's likeness gleams
Clearly etched.

5. *On Sacred Scripture*

O what spirit, what fiery whirlwind
Takes my bones and stirs
My deepest thoughts? When I was resting
Near my door not long ago,
And it was evening, did I
Swallow a falling star? And is it
Trying to escape, not knowing how
In this disgraceful lodging to be hidden?
Have I in sipping honey
Consumed the bee, in eating up
The house eaten up the mistress of the house?
Not bee, not star has penetrated me.
Most Holy Writ, it's you who've traveled through
All the dark nooks and hidden pleats
Of the heart, the alleys and the curves
Of flying passion. Ah, how wise and skilled you are
To slip through these paths, windings, knots.
The spirit that has reared the building
Knows it best.

VI. In pacem Britannicam

Anglia cur solùm fuso sine sanguine sicca est,
    Cùm natet in tantis caetera terra malis?
Sit licet in pelago semper, sine fluctibus illa est,
    Cùm qui plus terrae, plus habuere maris.
Naufragij causa est alijs mare, roboris Anglo,   5
    Et quae corrumpit moenia, murus aqua est.
Nempe hìc Religio floret, regina quietis,
    Túque super nostras, Christe, moueris aquas.

VII. Auaritia

Aurum nocte videns, vidisse insomnia dicit:
    Aurum luce videns, nulla videre putat.
O falsos homines! Vigilat, qui somniat aurum,
    Plúsque habet hic laetus, quàm vel Auarus habet.

VIII. In Lotionem pedum Apostolorum

Solem ex Oceano Veteres exurgere fingunt
    Postquam se gelidis nocte refecit aquis:

6. On the British peace

Why is England dry
(Not having poured her blood out),
While all the earth wades
Through tides of evil?
Though she is always in the sea,
She has no waves; at the same time,
They who have more land more sea possess.
The sea is the cause of shipwreck to them;
To England, a source of strength—
And water, which wrecks walls, is itself a wall.
For sure Religion flowers here, the Queen of Peace,
And you, Christ, move upon our waters.

7. Avarice

Gold seen at night is said
To be a dream,
And in the light is thought
To be real. O vain
Men, he is awake who dreams
Of gold: he's got more gold than even
The avaricious man.

8. On the washing of the apostles' feet

The ancients believed the sun
Heaved up out of the sea

Veriùs hoc olim factum est, vbi, Christe, lauares
Illos, qui mundum circumiere, pedes.

IX. In D. Lucam

Cur Deus elegit Medicum, qui numine plenus
Diuinâ Christi scriberet acta manu?
Vt discat sibi quisque, quid vtile: nempe nocebat
Crudum olim pomum, tristis Adame, tibi.

X. Papae titulus, Nec Deus Nec Homo

Quisnam Antichristus cessemus quaerere; Papa
Nec Deus est nec Homo: Christus vterque fuit.

XI. Tributi solutio

Piscis tributum soluit; & tu Caesari:
Vtrumque mirum est: hoc tamen mirum magìs,
Quòd omnibus tute imperes, nemo tibi.

After he'd refreshed himself
At night in ice-cold water.
This was truer long ago
When you, Christ, bathed those feet
Which made their way around the world.

9. *On Luke the doctor*

Why did God a doctor pick,
That he, filled up with the Holy Spirit,
Might with his consecrated hand
Record the acts of Christ?
It was in order that each man
Might learn what's good for him.
Surely the unripened fruit of old
Was agony for you, unlucky Adam.

10. *The Pope's title (not God or man)*

Let us not continue asking
Who is the Antichrist. The Pope is not
God or man: Christ was both.

11. *The payment of tribute*

The fish gives up the coin,
And you give that to Caesar:
Both these acts are strange,

XII. *Tempestas Christo dormiente*

Cum dormis, surgit pelagus: cùm, Christe, resurgis,
  Dormitat pelagus: Quàm bene fraena tenes!

XIII. *Bonus Ciuis*

Sagax Humilitas, eligens viros bonos
Atque euehens, bonum facit faecundius,
Quàm si ipse solus omnia interuerteret,
Suámque in alijs possidet prudentiam.

XIV. *In Vmbram Petri*

Produxit Vmbram corpus, Vmbra corpori
  Vitam reduxit: ecce gratitudinem.

But the second is the stranger,
For you of everyone
Are uncontested king,
While no one is of you.

12. *The storm, while Christ sleeps*

While you sleep the sea arises:
When, Christ, you rise up again,
The sea slumbers. How well
You master things!

13. *The good citizen*

Shrewd humility, picking out
And making prominent the good
Man, makes that good one richer
Then if he alone
Were appropriating everything. She shows
Her prudence through another's acts.

14. *On Peter's shadow*

The body made a shadow;
The shadow to the body
Gave life back: Mark in that
A complementary deed.

XV. Martha: Maria

Christus adest: crebris aedes percurrite scopis,
    Excutite aulaea, & luceat igne focus.
Omnia purgentur, niteat mihi tota supellex,
    Parcite luminibus, sítque lucerna domus:
O cessatrices! eccum puluisculus illic!   5
    Corde tuo forsan, caetera munda, SOROR.

XVI. Amor

Quid metuant homines infrà, supráue minentur
    Sydera, pendenti sedulus aure bibis:
Vtque ouis in dumis, haeres in crine Cometae,
    Sollicitus, ne te stella perita notet:
Omnia quaerendo, sed te, super omnia, vexas: 5
    Et quid tu tandem desidiosus? AMO.

15. *Martha; Mary*

"Christ is here. Sweep up the rooms,
Shake out the curtains, let a fire
Light the hearth. All should be clean,
Every stick of furniture
Should be bright, I say; go easy
With the lights: let the house itself
Be a lamp. Oh, slowpokes!
Look, there's still
Some fine dust here!"
"Perhaps in your heart, Sister.
All else is clean."

16. *Love*

What men are frightened of
Below, or what the stars'
Influence above makes dangerous,
You, on the lookout, drink
In with your ear, bending it
Down. As a sheep
In briars, you are tangled
In the hair of the comet,
Worried that a cunning star
May see you there. All things
You vex by being curious of them.
But above all things you vex yourself.
But why so sluggish? Look at me!
I'm in love.

XVII. In Superbum

Magnas es; esto. Bulla si vocaberis,
Largiar & istud: scilicet Magnatibus
Difficilis esse haud soleo: nam, pol, si forem,
Ipsi sibi sunt nequiter facillimi.
Quin, mitte nugas; téque carnem & sanguinem   5
Communem habere crede cum Cerdonibus:
Illum volo, qui calceat lixam tuum.

XVIII. In eundem

Unusquisque hominum, Terra est; & filius arui.
   Dic mihi, mons sterilis, vallis an vber eris?

XIX. Afflictio

Quos tu calcasti fluctus, me, Christe, lacessunt,
   Transiliúntque caput, qui subiere pedes.
Christe, super fluctus si non discurrere detur:
   Per fluctus saltem, fac, precor, ipse vadem.

17. *On the proud man*

You're a personage: so let it be.
If by "bubble" you'll be called,
I'll flatter you with that.
To be sure, with personages
I'm not accustomed to be saucy.
Indeed, if I should be so,
They'd still be with themselves
Most vilely lenient. Rather, let's
Quit this nonsense: believe you're
Blood-relative to cobblers—
I mean the kind who fit
Shoes on your servants.

18. *On the same*

Each man is earth, and the field's child. Tell me,
Will you be a sterile mountain or a fertile valley?

19. *Affliction*

Those waves you walked upon,
My Lord, and which come up to
Your feet, pound and leap above
My head. Christ, if I can't go
On top of the water, let me at least,
I beg you, pass through the waves.

XX. In κενοδοξίαν

Qui sugit auido spiritu rumusculos
Et flatulentas aucupatur glorias,
Foelicitatis culmen extra se locat,
Spargítque per tot capita, quot vulgus gerit.
Tu verò collige te, tibíque insistito,   5
Breuiore nodo stringe vitae sarcinas,
Rotundus in te: namque si ansatus sies,
Te mille rixae, mille prensabunt doli,
Ducéntque, donec incidentem in cassidem
Te mille nasi, mille rideant sinus.   10
Quare, peritus nauta, vela contrahas,
Famámque nec difflaueris, nec suxeris:
Tuásque librans actiones, gloriam
Si ducat agmen, reprime; sin claudat, sinas.
Morosus, oxygala est: leuis, coagulum.   15

XXI. In Gulosum

Dum prono rapis ore cibos, & fercula verris,
   Intra extráque graui plenus es illuuie.
Non iam ventriculus, verùm spelunca vocetur
   Illa cauerna, in quâ tot coiere ferae.

20. On vainglory

Who with a greedy spirit sucks
Idle rumor, and after huffing glories chases,
Puts the essential joy beyond his reach,
And dissipates it among as many heads
As there are in the common crowd.
Pull yourself together, shift for yourself,
And bind with a tighter knot
The loads of life, till you are self-contained.
For if you stick your neck out,
A thousand frauds, a thousand sorrows will
Grip and pull you; and when you've stumbled into
An embarrassing position,
A thousand breasts and noses rock with laughter.
And so, as an experienced sailor, pull in your sails;
Don't let your fame be loose, don't suck it in too much;
Be moderate in what you do. If glory
Leads the column, rein it in; if it
Lags behind, let it loose.
Moroseness has a curdlike thickness,
And giddiness is rennet-thin.

21. On the glutton

While you shovel food
In your swooping mouth
And pick clean whole trays,
You are weighted down within
And without with a flood

Ipse fruare, licet, solus graueolente sepulcro;
   Te petet, ante diem quisquis obire cupit.

XXII. In Improbum disertum

Sericus est dictis, factis pannusia Baucis:
   Os & lingua tibi diues, egena manus:
Ni facias, vt opes linguae per brachia serpant,
   Aurea pro naulo lingua Charontis erit.

XXIII. Consolatio

Cur lacrymas & tarda trahis suspiria, tanquam
   Nunc primùm socij mors foret atra tui?
Nos autem, à cunis, omnes sententia Mortis
   Quotidie iugulat, nec semel vllus obit.
Viuimus in praesens: hesternam viuere vitam   5
   Nemo potest: hodie vita sepulta prior.
Trecentos obijt Nestor, non transijt annos,
   Vel quia tot moritur, tot viguisse probes.

Of dirt. That deep hole—
Don't just call it belly now,
But cavern, in which so many
Fierce beasts have been packed together.
You alone can take pleasure
In a tomb's stench. He will visit you
Who wants to be interred before his time.

22. *On the eloquence of the wicked*

Your words are silk, your deeds
The clothes of Baucis:[1] rich
Your mouth and tongue, poor
Your hand. Unless the tongue's
Soul creep down your arm,
Your gilded talk will be
Charon's passage money.

23. *Consolation*

Why do you weep and heave
Long-drawn-out sighs, as though the hooded death
Of your friend were but now arrived?
For from our cradles the decree of death
Daily murders all of us,
And no one dies just once. We live
For the present: no one can live
The life that was the day before.
The old life is buried now.

Dum lacrymas, it vita: tuus tibi clepsydra fletus,
    Et numerat mortes singula gutta pares;   10
Frustra itaque in tot funeribus miraberis vnum,
    Sera nimis lacryma haec, si lacrymabis, erit.
Siste tuum fletum & gemitus: namque imbribus istis
    Ac zephyris, carnis flos remeare nequit.
Nec tu pro socio doleas, qui fugit ad illud   15
    Culmen, vbi pro te nemo dolere potest.

XXIV. In Angelos

Intellectus adultus Angelorum
Haud nostro similis, cui necesse,
Vt dentur species, rogare sensum:
Et ni lumina ianuam resignent,
Et nostrae tribuant molae farinam,   5
Saepe ex se nihil otiosa cudit.
A nobis etenim procul remoti
Labuntur fluuij scientiarum:
Si non per species, nequimus ipsi,
Quid ipsi sumus, assequi putando.   10
Non tantum est iter Angelis ad vndas,

Nestor died—he did not live—
Three hundred years;
No one could say he flourished
All those deathward years.
While you weep, life moves:
Your tears are your water clock,
And each drop counts one death.
But among all those deaths you will
Question the single death in vain.
And these tears will be, if you
Weep, too late. Leave off your tears
And sighs: for by these rains and winds
The bud of mortal life cannot return.
For a comrade, who flies
To that height where no one can
Weep for you, do not shed tears.

24. *On angels*

The perfected mind of angels
Is not like ours at all,
Which must by nature
Look to our senses
For concrete images.
Eyes must unlock
The outer world, and to our mills
Yield grain; of itself the mind
Often will grind out, being slow,
No bounty. Far off indeed
From us do knowledge's obscure
Streams descend: if it weren't

Nullo circuitu scienda pungunt,
Illis perpetuae patent fenestrae,
Se per se facili modo scientes,
Atque ipsi sibi sunt mola & farina.   15

XXV. Roma, Anagr.
(Oram, Maro, Ramo, Armo, Mora, Amor)

ROMA, tuum nomen quam non pertransijt ORAM,
   Cùm Latium ferrent secula prisca iugum?
Non deerat vel fama tibi, vel carmina famae,
   Vnde MARO laudes duxit ad astra tuas.
At nunc exucco similis tua gloria RAMO   5
   A veteri trunco & nobilitate cadit.
Laus antiqua & honor perijt: quasi scilicet ARMO
   Te deiecissent tempora longa suo.
Quin tibi tam desperatae MORA nulla medetur,
   Quâ Fabio quondam sub duce nata salus.   10
Hinc te olim gentes miratae odere vicissim;
   Et cum sublatâ laude recedit AMOR.

For concrete things, we ourselves
Could not by thinking find
What we are in ourselves.
To the water angels don't have to travel
So far: they can be roused
By knowledge that is not
Roundabout; to them
Eternal windows are open;
By virtue of themselves they have
An easy way to know themselves; they are
To themselves both grain and mill.

25. *Rome: an anagram (frontier, Maro, branch, shoulder, delay, love)*

Rome, what *frontier* did your name
Not cross, when times of old endured
The Latin yoke? Fame you did not lack,
Nor songs of fame, whence *Maro*
Made you eminent among the stars.
But now your glory like a withered *branch*
From an old and noble tree is fallen.
Ancient praise and honor are no more, as if
From their *shoulder* distant times
Had thrown you down. Indeed for you *delay*
Does not mend despair,
As once beneath the hand of Fabius[2]
Delay produced security. Hence the nations now,
Whose admiration you possessed,
Hate you in turn:
When praise decays, *love* departs.

XXVI. *Vrbani VIII Pont. Respons.*

Cum Romam nequeas, quod aues, euertere, nomen
    Inuertis, mores carpis & obloqueris:
Te Germana tamen pubes, te Graecus & Anglus
    Arguit, exceptos quos pia Roma fouet:
Hostibus haec etiam parcens imitatur Iesum.   5
    Inuertis nomen. Quid tibi dicit? AMOR.

XXVII. *Respons. ad Vrb. VIII*

Non placet vrbanus noster de nomine lusus
    Romano, sed res seria Roma tibi est:
Nempe Caput Romae es, cuius mysteria velles
    Esse iocum soli, plebe stupente, tibi:
Attamen VRBANI delecto nomine, constat   5
    Quàm satur & suauis sit tibi Roma iocus.

XXVIII. *Ad Vrbanum VIII Pont.*

Pontificem tandem nacta est sibi Roma poetam:
    Res redit ad vates, Pieriósque duces:
Quod Bellarminus nequijt, fortasse poetae

26. The response of Pope Urban VIII

Since you can't, as you would like,
Demolish Rome, you change her name,
Slander and abuse her customs.
The young German, Greek, and Englishman
Call you down; and holy Rome, who took them in,
Loves them. Also, in forgiving her enemies, she imitates
Jesus. Invert the name. What does it tell you?
"I am loved."

27. Response to Urban VIII

Our urbane game about the Roman name
Does not please you,
But Rome herself concerns you very much.
For sure you are the head of Rome,
The mysteries of whom you would
Like to make a private joke of,
With cowlike commoners around.
Still, with Urban your chosen name, to you for sure
How rich and sweet a jest is Rome.

28. To Pope Urban VIII

Rome has found herself at last
A poet pope. Governance returns to bards,
To inspired kings. What Bellarmine[3] could not,
Perhaps the poet will

Suauiter efficient, absque rigore Scholae.
Cedito Barbaries: Helicon iam litibus instat,   5
    Squalorémque togae candida Musa fugat.

XXIX. Λογικὴ Θυσία

Ararúmque Hominúmque ortum si mente pererres,
    Cespes viuus, Homo; mortuus, Ara fuit:
Quae diuisa nocent, Christi per foedus, in vnum
    Conueniunt; & Homo viua fit Ara Dei.

XXX. *In Thomam Didymum*

Dum te vel digitis minister vrget,
Et hoc indicium subis, Redemptor?
Nempe es totus amor, medulla amoris,
Qui spissae fidei breuíque menti
Paras hospitium torúmque dulcem,   5
Quô se condat & implicet volutans
Ceu fidâ statione & arce certâ,
Ne perdat Leo rugiens vagantem.

In sweetness and without the scholar's rigor
Bring about? Yield, barbarians!
Already Helicon menaces the courts,
And the white-robed Muse chases off
The dirty toga.

29. *Reasonable sacrifice*

If one considers the rise of men and altars,
Earth breathed upon was man, dead earth
An altar. These, which separated
From one another make for harm, through Christ's
    compacts
Were put together: so man becomes
The living altar of God.

30. *On Thomas Didymus*

The servant puts his fingers in you.
Do you, Redeemer, permit this sign?
For sure you are all love, and the pith of it.
You make a shelter and a sweet rest
For a grudging faith and a narrow mind,
In which, luxuriating, they may conceal
And wrap themselves
As in a good inn or a strong fort,
Before a roaring lion eats
Them as they wander.

XXXI. In Solarium

Coniugium Caeli Terraéque haec machina praestat;
    Debetur Caelo lumen, & vmbra solo:
Sic Hominis moles animâque & corpore constat,
    Cuius ab oppositis fluxit origo locis.
Contemplare, miser, quantum terroris haberet   5
    Vel sine luce solum, vel sine mente caro.

XXXII. Triumphus Mortis

O mea suspicienda manus, ventérque perennis!
Quem non Emathius torrens, non sanguine pinguis
Daunia, non satiat bis ter millesima caedis
Progenies, mundíque aetas abdomine nostro
Ingluuiéque minor. Quercus habitare feruntur   5
Prisci, crescentésque vnà cum prole cauernas:
Nec tamen excludor: namque vnâ ex arbore vitam
Glans dedit, & truncus tectum, & ramalia mortem.
   Confluere intereà passim ad Floralia pubes
Coeperat, agricolis mentémque & aratra solutis: 10
Compita feruescunt pedibus, clamoribus aether.
Hìc vbi discumbunt per gramina, salsior vnus

31. *On the sundial*

This machine shows
Earth and heaven linked.
It owes its light to heaven,
Its shadow to the ground.
Thus man's weight and import
Hangs between a body
And a spirit: the source of man
From opposite directions flowed.
Wretch, meditate on this:
How frightened the ground
Would be without the light,
Or the flesh without the mind.

32. *The triumph of Death*

Ah, awesome hand, eternal belly
Which the River Peneus, Daunia[4] gross with blood,
And slaughter's countless children do not stuff—
Gut older than the world with greed!

Men lived in oak trees long ago,
And caves larger as their children grew.
Still they couldn't shut it out:
For from a single tree the acorn yielded
Life, the trunk a house, the branches death.

And then from here, from there, youths, planters
Loosed from worry and the plow, began

Omnia suspendit naso, sociósque lacessit:
Non fert Vcalegon, atque amentata retorquet
Dicta ferox: haerent lateri conuitia fixo.   15
Scinditur in partes vulgus ceu compita: telum
Ira facit, mundúsque ipse est apotheca furoris.
Liber alit rixas: potantibus omnia bina
Sunt, praeter vitam: saxis hic sternitur, alter
Ambustis sudibus: pars vitam in pocula fundunt,   20
In patinas alij: furit inconstantia vini
Sanguine, quem dederat, spolians. Primordia Mortis
Haec fuerant: sic Tisiphone virguncula lusit.
   Non placuit rudis atque ignara occisio: Morti
Quaeritur ingenium, doctúsque homicida probatur.   25
Hinc tyrocinium, paruóque assueta iuuentus,
Fictáque Bellona & verae ludibria pugnae,
Instructaéque acies, hyemésque in pellibus actae,
Omniáque haec vt transadigant sine crimine costas,
Artificésque necis clueant, & mortis alumni.   30
Nempe & millenos ad palum interficit hostes
Assiduus tyro, si sit spectanda voluntas.
Heu miseri! Quis tantùm ipsis virtutibus instat
Quantùm caedi? adeón' vnam vos pascere vitam,
Perdere sexcentas? crescit tamen hydra nocendi   35
Tristis, vbi ac ferrum tellure reciditur imâ,
Faecundúsque chalybs sceleris, iam sanguine tinctus,
Expleri nequit, & totum depascitur Orbem.
Quid memorem tormenta, quibus prius horruit aeuum;
Balistásque Onagrósque & quicquid Scorpio saeuus   40
Vel Catapulta potest, Siculíque inuenta magistri,
Anglorúmque arcus gaudentes sanguine Galli,
Fustibalos fundásque, quibus, cum Numine, fretus

To come together for the feasts of Flora.
Crossroads grew hot with feet, the air with cries.
Here, when they lay about the grass,
One more nervy than the rest
Turned up his nose, dared his friends.
His neighbor wouldn't bear it; a savage fellow, he
Hurled words back like javelins: insults
Stuck in the pierced side. The crowd like a
Forked road divided. Anger
Made a weapon, the world itself
Was the arsenal of rage. Bacchus made for fights:
With those who drank, all things were double
But life: one was felled by stones, another
With a firebrand: some poured out
Life in a cup, others into dishes: skittish wine
Raged, plundering the blood
It had enriched. These were Death's beginnings;
So Tisiphone, a little girl, amused herself.
Killing, unrefined, rude, was not enough: a talent
For death was sought, and the learned killer
Came into vogue. And so recruits, young men
Used to scanty rations, makeshift Goddess of War[5]
And the sports of authentic war, battle lines
Deployed, winters braved in skins—all these
That men might gouge unblamed through ribs
And get their fame as the artisans
And graduates of death. Certainly
A rew recruit who keeps at it in practice tilts can kill
A thousand adversaries, if his desire counts.

Ah, sad men, who so much as death's
Is virtue's servant? Surely not to feed one life
Six hundred lives need end.

Strauit Idumaeum diuinus Tityrus hostem?
Adde etiam currus, & cum temone Britanno   45
Aruiragum, falcésque obstantia quaeque metentes.
Quin Aries ruit, & multâ Demetrius arte:
Sic olim cecidere.
    Deerat adhuc vitijs hominum dignissima mundo
Machina, quam nullum satìs execrabitur aeuum;   50
Liquitur ardenti candens fornace metallum,
Fusáque decurrit notis aqua ferrea sulcis:
Exoritur tubus, atque instar Cyclopis Homeri
Luscum prodigium, medióque foramine gaudens.
Inde rotae atque axes subeunt, quasi sella curulis   55
Quâ Mors ipsa sedens hominum de gente triumphat.
Accedit Pyrius puluis, laquearibus Orci
Erutus, infernae pretiosa tragemata mensae,
Sulphureóque lacu, totâque imbuta Mephiti.
Huic Glans adijcitur (non quam ructare vetustas   60
Creditur, ante satas prono cum numine fruges)
Plumbea glans, liuensque suae quasi conscia noxae,
Purpureus lictor Plutonis, epistola Fati
Plumbis obsignata, colósque & stamina vitae
Perrumpens, Atropi vetulae marcentibus vlnis.   65
    Haec vbi iuncta, subit viuo cum fune minister,
Fatalémque leuans dextram, quâ stupeus ignis
Mulcetur vento, accendit cum fomite partem
Pulueris inferni; properat datus ignis, & omnem
Materiam vexat: nec iam se continet antro   70
Tisiphone; flammâ & fallaci fulmine cincta
Euolat, horrendúmque ciet bacchata fragorem.
It stridor, caelósque omnes & Tartara findit.
Non iam exaudiri quicquam vel Musica caeli

Still violence' dark hydra, even
When its iron veins are wrenched from the deep earth,
Flourishes, and the steel of evil, already
Dyed with blood, cannot be satisfied
And devours all the world.
Why remember siege machines
Which terrified a former time—
What all of them can do: catapults, Archimedes'
Inventions, the English bow rejoicing in the blood of
    France,
The sling by which, by the will of God,
Immortal David knocked Goliath down?
Add to these the chariot, and Arviragus, the Briton king,
Fighting on a wagon shaft, and sickles
Mowing down whatever stands before them.
The battering ram, and Demetrius,[6]
Artisan of sieges, rushed forth indeed:
So carnage was of old.

Still the world had not the engine
Most worthy of the sins of men.
No age will swear at it enough: metal glowing
In the red kiln liquifies, and bubbling down
In the worn grooves, the iron-water pours:
The tube emerges, and the monster
With a single eye, in the likeness
Of Homer's Cyclops, rejoices in the hole bored
In the middle. Then wheels and axles take the burden up
Like a curule chair, and from it
Death, sitting, triumphs over man.
On top of this there's red-hot dust
Erupting from the panelled ceilings of the dead
(Select desserts for Hades' table), and from the Sulphur
    Lake

Vel gemitus Erebi: piceo se turbine voluens   75
Totámque eructans nubem, Glans proruit imo
Praecipitata; cadunt vrbes, formidine muri
Diffugiunt, fragilísque crepant coenacula mundi.
Strata iacent toto millena cadauera campo
Vno ictu: non sic pestis, non stella maligno   80
Afflatu perimunt: en, Cymba Cocytia turbis
Ingemit, & defessus opem iam Portitor orat.
Nec Glans sola nocet; mortem quandoque susurrat
Aura volans, vitámque aer, quam pauerat, aufert.

  Dicite, vos Furiae, quâ gaudet origine Monstrum.   85
Nox Aetnam, noctémque Chaos genuere priores.
Aetna Cacum igniuomum dedit, hic Ixiona multis
Cantatum; deinde Ixion cum nubibus atris
Congrediens genuit Monachum, qui limen opacae
Triste colens cellae, noctúque & Daemone plenum,   90
Protulit horrendum hoc primus cum puluere monstrum.
Quis Monachos mortem meditari, & puluere tristi
Versatos neget, atque humiles, queîs talia cordi
Tam demissa, ipsámque adeò subeuntia terram?

  Nec tamen hìc noster stetit impetus: exilit omni   95
Tormento peior Iesuita, & fulminat Orbem,
Ridens Bombardas miseras, quae corpora perdunt
Non animas, raróque ornantur sanguine regum
Obstreperae stulto sonitu, criménque fatentes.

  Imperij hìc culmen figo: mortalibus actum est   100
Corporéque atque animo. Totus mihi seruiat Orbis.

With all Mephitis[7] tainted; plus the acorn
(Not the one it's said the ancients belched
Before they learned to till and reap with God's
      assistance),
The special one, a nut of lead, black, as if aware
Of its guilt, Dis's purple lictor, Fate's
Short note sealed up in lead, ripping through
The distaffs and the threads of life
Now that the arms of withered Atropos
Are weak. When these things have been assembled
A lackey with a living fuse approaches, and lifting
His fatal hand to make the oakum fire
Flutter in the wind, ignites
A shred of hell's ash with the tinder; the fire, put to it,
Hurries on, and vexes the stuff;
In her hole Tisiphone confines herself no longer;
Girded up with fire and deceitful lightning,
She rushes out, and her revelling arouses
A frightening din. A whine is emitted, splits
Tartarus and all the heavens. Now nothing
Of celestial music or the groans of hell
Is heard: spinning in a pitch-
Black whirlwind, and vomiting a whole cloud,
The cannonball, shot up
From deep below, roars out; cities collapse, walls
Fly apart, and the upper regions of the fragile world
Quake. With but a shot, a thousand corpses lie
Prostrate on the field: the plague, the stars
That breathe ill luck, do not destroy like this:
Indeed the boat of Cocytus mutters
With disordered crowds, and the tired pilot begs
For help. Not only does the gun's nut wound:
Since the circling wind now whispers death,

The air removes the life it once upheld.

Tell me, Furies, from what beginning
The monster builds his joy. Chaos
Fashioned darkness, and darkness Aetna.
Aetna yielded up the fire-breathing Cacus[8]
Who bred Ixion, whom many sing about;
And then commingling with an inky cloud, Ixion
Produced a monk, who, living in a dark
Cell's unjoyous doorway full of demons
And of night, first invented
This terrifying freak with powder.
Who denies that monks are taken up with death;
That they grovel in the joyless dust; that they prize
In their hearts humiliating things like this—indeed
Things that go beneath the earth itself?

Still Death's strength is not exhausted here.
A Jesuit arises worse than any
Siege machine, and with his lightnings
Intimidates the world, laughing at
The wretched cannons clamorous with stupid noise
Confessing guilt, which annihilate the body
But not the spirit, and are decorated by the vintage
Blood of kings.
                    The summit of his power Death
Fixes here; he is the certain end
Of mortals in the flesh and spirit;
And to him all the world must be enslaved.

XXXIII. *Triumphus Christiani: in Mortem*

Ain' verò? quanta praedicas? hercle aedepol,
Magnificus es screator, homicida inclytus.
Quid ipse faciam? qui nec arboreas sudes
In te, nec arcus, scorpionésue, aut rotas,
Gladiósue, Catapultásue teneam, quin neque   5
Alapas nec Arietes? Quid ergo? Agnum & Crucem.

XXXIV. *In Johannem* ἐπιστήθιον

Ah nunc, helluo, fac, vt ipse sugam:
Num totum tibi pectus imputabis?
Fontem intercipis omnibus patentem?
Quin pro me quoque sanguinem profudit,
Et ius pectoris inde consecutus   5
Lac cum sanguine posco deuolutum;
Vt, si gratia tanta copuletur
Peccati veniae mei, vel ipsos
Occumbens humero Thronos lacessam.

33. *The Christian's triumph: against Death*

O what wonders do you prophesy?
You are the great
Clarion, the famous doom of man.
What shall I do—
I, who bear against you
No spears or bows, no shot
Or wheels, no swords
Or cannons, indeed
No fists or battering rams?
What can I use against you?
The Lamb, the cross.

34. *To John, leaning on the Lord's breast*

Ah now, glutton, let me suck too!
You won't really hoard the whole
Breast for yourself! Do you thieve
Away from everyone that common well?
He also shed his blood for me,
And thus, having rightful
Access to the breast, I claim the milk
Mingled with the blood. And then,
If so much grace is intermixed
To wash my sin away, I,
Falling dead, will with my shoulder
Rock those royal heights.

XXXV. *Ad Dominum*

Christe, decus, dulcedo, & centum circiter Hyblae,
    Cordis apex, animae pugnáque páxque meae,
Quin, sine, te cernam; quoties iam dixero, cernam;
    Immoriárque oculis, o mea vita, tuis.
Si licet, immoriar: vel si tua visio vita est,   5
    Cur sine te, votis immoriturus, ago?
Ah, cernam; Tu, qui caecos sanare solebas,
    Cùm te non videam, méne videre putas?
Non video, certum est iurare; aut si hoc vetuisti,
    Praeuenias vultu non facienda tuo.   10

35. *To the Lord*

Christ, bright one, sweet one, more like
A hundred fabled honey-bearing towns,
Heart's highest seat, the war
Of my spirit, and its peace—
O let me see you! As often
As I say it, I will see you.
In your eyes, O my life, I will die.
If I can, I will die in them; or if,
By virtue of your gaze, life lives,
Why, on the point of death
In my devotions, do I live without you?
Ah, I will see. You, who always healed
The blind, when I see you not, do you think
I see at all? On my determined oath,
I do not see; or, if you've forbidden swearing,
Prevent it with your countenance!

Memoriae Matris Sacrum

I.

Ah Mater, quo te deplorem fonte? Dolores
    Quae guttae poterunt enumerare meos?
Sicca meis lacrymis Thamesis vicina videtur,
    Virtutúmque choro siccior ipse tuo.
In flumen moerore nigrum si funderer ardens,   5
    Laudibus haud fierem sepia iusta tuis.
Tantùm istaec scribo gratus, ne tu mihi tantùm
    Mater: & ista Dolor nunc tibi Metra parit.

II.

Corneliae sanctae, graues Semproniae,
Et quicquid vspiam est seuerae foeminae,
Conferte lacrymas: Illa, quae vos miscuit

In Sacred Memory of My Mother[1]

1.

Ah, Mother, is there a fountain
To pour the tears I have for you?
Are there as many drops of liquid
As there are sorrows in me?
Thames is dry compared with what I weep,
And I am nothing to the tears
Your virtues' choir sheds. If burning up I were
Poured out to make a river dark with grieving,
The honor due you would from me
Get no fitting ink to give it.
With thanks I write these things alone—
You my mother, mine alone: mourning
Now creates these poems for you.

2.

Grave and holy women, Cornelian,
Sempronian—every sober woman—
Come here to weep: she who

Vestrásque laudes, poscit & mixtas genas.
Namque hanc ruinam salua Grauitas defleat,   5
Pudórque constet vel solutis crinibus;
Quandoque vultûs sola maiestas, Dolor.

   Decus mulierum perijt: & metuunt viri
Vtrumque sexum dote ne mulctauerit.
Non illa soles terere comptu lubricos,   10
Struices superbas atque turritum caput
Molita, reliquum deinde garriens diem
(Nam post Babelem linguae adest confusio)
Quin post modestam, qualis integras decet,
Substructionem capitis & nimbum breuem,   15
Animam recentem rite curauit sacris
Adorta numen acri & igneâ prece.

   Dein familiam lustrat, & res prandij,
Horti, colíque distributim pensitat.
Suum cuique tempus & locus datur.   20
Inde exiguntur pensa crudo vespere.
Ratione certâ vita constat & domus,
Prudenter inito quot-diebus calculo.
Totâ renident aede decus & suauitas
Animo renidentes priùs. Sin rarior   25
Magnatis appulsu extulit se occasio,
Surrexit vnà & illa, seséque extulit:
Occasione certat, imò & obtinet.
Proh! quantus imber, quanta labri comitas,
Lepos seuerus, Pallas mixta Gratijs;   30
Loquitur numellas, compedes & retia:
Aut si negotio hora sumenda est, rei
Per angiportus & maeandros labitur,
Ipsos Catones prouocans oraculis.

You and your honors mingled in her,
Calls for you to mingle tears.
Let perfect gravity for this
Wreckage mourn; modesty, even with
Unbound hair, contain herself: at times
Pain is a face's only noble look.
Dead now woman's glory,
And there's a fear in men she has
Left man and woman both
Without their heritage.
She did not deck herself so grandly she
Wasted time that glides away, nor did she
Pile up her hair as high as pride,
Then the day's remainder spend
In idle talk (language being chaos since
The time of Babel); but after doing up her hair
In a simple style, the way that decent women do,
And putting round the front a tiny ribbon,
She put her dewy soul in care
Of holy business, having with
Sharp and fiery prayer besieged the Lord.
She looks the household over, to luncheon gives,
And gardening, and sewing, the proper time
And place, balancing the need for each.
So the labor of the day is done
In the glow of dusk. House and living are
On tight reckoning established, started
Each day with skill, a clear calculation.
First the spirit bright, the sweet, the graceful,
Illuminate the whole house.
But if a rare occasion rose
By the coming of a person of importance
She rose along with it and met it.

Tum quanta tabulis artifex? quae scriptio?　　　³⁵
Bellum putamen, nucleus bellissimus,
Sententiae cum voce mirè conuenit,
Volant per orbem literae notissimae:
O blanda dextra, neutiquam istoc pulueris,
Quò nunc recumbis, scriptio merita est tua,　　　⁴⁰
Pactoli arena tibi tumulus est vnicus.

　Adde his trientem Musices, quae molliens
Mulcénsque dotes caeteras visa est quasi
Caelestis harmoniae breue praeludium.
Quàm mira tandem Subleuatrix pauperum!　　　⁴⁵
Languentium baculus, teges iacentium,
Commune cordis palpitantis balsamum:
Benedictiones publicae cingunt caput,
Caelíque referunt & praeoccupant modum.
Fatisco referens tanta quae numerant mei　　　⁵⁰
Solùm dolores, & dolores, stellulae.

　At tu qui ineptè haec dicta censes filio,
Nato parentis auferens Encomium,
Abito, trunce, cum tuis pudoribus.
Ergo ipse solùm mutus atque excors ero　　　⁵⁵
Strepente mundo tinnulis praeconijs?
Mihíne matris vrna clausa est vnico,
Herbae exoletae, ros-marinus aridus?
Matríne linguam refero, solùm vt mordeam?
Abito, barde. Quàm piè istic sum impudens!　　　⁶⁰
Tu verò mater perpetim laudabere
Nato dolenti: literae hoc debent tibi
Queîs me educasti; sponte chartas illinunt
Fructum laborum consecutae maximum
Laudando Matrem, cùm repugnant inscij.　　　⁶⁵

No occasion could unnerve her,
And from the start she had it in her grip.
Ah, this very storm, this very grace of speech,
Stern winsomeness, wit
And wisdom mixed! She holds a discourse
On hunting and the care of cattle; or if her duties
Take her for an hour, she eases through
Their twists and labyrinths, better than
Very Catos with her wise maxims.
And what a polished craftsman in her writing!
What kind of writing? Beauteous the shell,
Most beauteous the kernel—
Thought and word exactly in accord. Letters,
Talked of everywhere, wing through the world.
O comely hand, the dust you lie in now
Your writing skill cannot have earned;
Only golden sand of Pactolus[2] could be your barrow.
In addition there is music
Which, the sweet moderating influence
Upon all other talents, seems as it were to be
A tiny prelude of celestial music.
And last, it is a wonder
How she helped the poor—to those
Who drooped, a staff; to those who fell,
A coverlet; to those whose hearts were faint,
A perfumed oil, a panacea. Public
Honors wreathe her head, heaven
Echoes and anticipates the melody.
I'm tired now, tired telling
Varieties my pain alone can number,
Pain as various as stars.
But you who think a son's talk
An impropriety, and take away from him

III.

Cur splendes, O Phoebe? ecquid demittere matrem
    Ad nos cum radio tam rutilante potes?
At superat caput illa tuum, quantum ipsa cadauer
    Mens superat; corpus solùm Elementa tenent.
Scilicet id splendes: haec est tibi causa micandi,   5
    Et lucro apponis gaudia sancta tuo.
Verùm heus, si nequeas caelo demittere matrem,
    Sítque omnis motûs nescia tanta quies,
Fac radios saltem ingemines, vt dextera tortos
    Implicet, & matrem, matre manente, petam.   10

The right to praise his mother, hold,
Fool, your embarrassing tongue.
Shall I keep quiet this way all alone,
Puzzled, disconsolate,
When all the public dins and roars?
Is my mother's urn shut up to me alone,
Herbs shrunk, rosemary withered up?
Shall I never put my tongue in my
Mother's service but to bite it? Get out, you fool!
What shameless loyalty in saying this!
Ah, Mother, forever will your mourning child
Praise you; you taught me how to write,
That skill owes you praise, that skill, unloosed,
Floods the paper, having gathered labor's
Finest fruit in honoring a mother,
Though those who do not understand will not allow it.

3.

Why, O Sun, shed light? By so
Flame-gold a shaft can you my mother
Let down to us? And yet as much
As mind is more than corpse, so higher
Than you she is: flesh is in the charge
Of elements, and only it. Certainly your light
Means this, and this your source of light:
You count her joys in heaven something gained
By you. O yet if you my mother
Can't send down from heaven, if your
Huge immobility no motion knows,
Multiply your rays of light

IV.

Quid nugor calamo fauens?
Mater perpetuis vuida gaudijs,
  Horto pro tenui colit
Edenem Boreae flatibus inuium.
  Quin caeli mihi sunt mei,   5
Materni decus, & debita nominis,
  Dúmque his inuigilo frequens
Stellarum socius, pellibus exuor.
  Quare Sphaeram egomet meam
Connixus, digitis impiger vrgeo: 10
  Te, Mater, celebrans diu,
Noctu te celebrans luminis aemulo.
  Per te nascor in hunc globum
Exemplóque tuo nascor in alterum: 15
  Bis tu mater eras mihi,
Vt currat paribus gloria tibijs.

That I may wind and twist
My hands in them, and, my mother staying
Where she is, climb up to her.

4.

Why do I indulge my quill
In play? Rather than a humble garden,
My mother, dewy with those pleasures
That do not end, an Eden tills
Which the big breathing of the North Wind
Cannot enter. O heaven to me
My mother's name, the glory of it,
And what I owe to it. While I
Am sentinel to these, on many nights
The stars' companion, I leave
The province of my flesh. And so
Putting forth my energy
I energetically employ
My sphere: by day, by night
(The rival of the day) I make
A praise for you, my mother. It was
By you I came into the world; with you
To follow, I come into the next.
Two times you were a mother to me
That on two legs
Glory might advance.

V.

Horti, deliciae *Dominae,* marcescite tandem;
    Ornâstis capulum, nec superesse licet.
Ecce decus vestrum spinis horrescit, acutâ
    Cultricem reuocans anxietate manum:
Terram & funus olent flores: Dominaéque cadauer   5
    Contiguas stirpes afflat, eaéque rosas.
In terram violae capite inclinantur opaco,
    Quaéque domus Dominae sit, grauitate docent.
Quare haud vos hortos, sed coemeteria dico,
    Dum torus absentem quisque reponit heram.   10
Eugè, perite omnes; nec posthâc exeat vlla
    Quaesitum Dominam gemma vel herba suam.
Cuncta ad radices redeant, tumulósque paternos;
    (Nempe sepulcra Satis numen inempta dedit.)
Occidite; aut sanè tantisper viuite, donec   15
    Vespere ros maestis funus honestet aquis.

5.

Now, you gardens, wither, gardens
That made your mistress happy.
You have adorned the coffin, you cannot now
Stay fresh. See how your brightness sprouts
Thorns, with sharp anxiety
Calling back the gardener.
Of earth, of corpse, flowers
Make their perfume; the mistress'
Body puts its breath upon
The stems about it, and they distill
Their breath upon the roses. Violets'
Dark heads bend to ground to show by heaviness
Where the mistress' dwelling is.
And so I call you resting places,
Not gardens now, while her,
No longer here, each flowerbed
Brings back. Good work! Now die,
All of you. Let not, after this,
Any herb or bud arise
To find its mistress. All things,
As one, must to their roots go back,
And to the humps of earth that fathered them.
In truth, God has made a free gift
Of sepulchers to them. Decay,
Or live until, when evening comes,
Dew dark drops of honor pours
Upon the corpse.

VI.

Galene, frustra es, cur miserum premens
Tot quaestionum fluctibus obruis,
   Arterias tractans micantes
      Corporeae fluidaéque molis?
Aegroto mentis: quam neque pixides   5
Nec tarda possunt pharmaca consequi,
   Vtrumque si praederis Indum,
      Vltrà animus spatiatur exlex.
Impos medendi, occidere si potes,
Nec sic parentem ducar ad optimam: 10
   Ni sanctè, vtì mater, recedam,
      Morte magìs viduabor illâ.
Quin cerne vt erres, inscie, brachium
Tentando sanum: si calet, aestuans,
   Ardore scribendi calescit,   15
      Mater inest saliente venâ.
Si totus infler, si tumeam crepax,
Ne membra culpes, causa animo latet
   Qui parturit laudes parentis:
      Nec grauidis medicina tuta est.   20
Irregularis nunc habitus mihi est:
Non exigatur crasis ad alterum.
   Quod tu febrem censes, salubre est
      Atque animo medicatur vnum.

6.

Vanity, O Galen, your work.
Why do you engulf me, pressing me,
Who have no joy, with all
These waves and waves of questions,
Poking at the beating arteries
Of a heap of flesh and liquid? My mind
Has a sickness: no box of balm,
No lazy medicines can come
Unto it. Though one should sack
India, and Indies too, the spirit
In anarchy flies out of reach.
You cannot cure, and if
You could give even death, I would
To my unequaled mother get
No ushering. If as she
I in holiness do not depart,
By death the more will I
Be robbed of her. Nothing
Wise, look, you miss it all by taking
The measure of an arm
That has no ill: if with heat
Inflamed, it builds its fires up
By writing's fever—the beating vein
My mother's residence. If all
Puffed up am I, if I grow large
And creak, put no limbs to blame,
For spirit, whose issue is
A mother's honoring, contains the source:
For pregnancy no medicine
Is safe. Not sure my state:

VII.

Pallida materni Genij atque exanguis imago,
In nebulas similésque tui res gaudia nunquid
Mutata? & pro matre mihi phantasma dolosum
Vberáque aerea hiscentem fallentia natum?
Vae nubi pluuiâ grauidae, non lacte, meásque   5
Ridenti lacrymas quibus vnis concolor vnda est.
Quin fugias? mea non fuerat tam nubila Iuno,
Tam segnis facies aurorae nescia vernae,
Tam languens genitrix cineri supposta fugaci:
Verùm augusta parens, sanctum os caelóque locandum, 10
Quale paludosos iamiam lictura recessus
Praetulit Astraea, aut solio Themis alma vetusto
Pensilis, atque acri dirimens Examine lites.
Hunc vultum ostendas, & tecum, nobile spectrum,
Quod superest vitae, insumam: Solísque iugales   15
Ipse tuae solùm adnectam, sine murmure, thensae.
Nec querar ingratos, studijs dum tabidus insto,
Effluxisse dies, suffocatámue Mineruam,
Aut spes productas, barbatáque somnia vertam
In vicium mundo sterili, cui cedo cometas   20
Ipse suos tanquam digno pallentiáque astra.
      Est mihi bis quinis laqueata domuncula tignis

My quality of flesh is not another's.
Do not, as if it were, prescribe.
Not ill what you interpret as
Ill heat, but the only thing that heals the heart.

7.

My mother's guardian spirit's
Pale and bloodless ghost,
Has joy been dissolved to mists
And things like you? No mother,
But spectre that lies to me—
Is that what you are? Your breasts,
Composed of air, untrue to me
Your child with an open mouth—
Are these what I possess? Cursed be the cloud
Weighed down with rain, not milk—
Cloud that makes my tears its joke,
My tears that only with the water have
A common tint. Begone, you ghost, for how will you
Remain intact? Not so made of mist my Juno was,
Not so much a snail that she did not
Know the morning's freshness,
Not so listless a mother broken
To dust that flies: no, a royal mother,
Her face for heaven fitted, Astraea's[3] face
Just before she went away from
Her fens of solitude, or Themis-like,[4]
The lenient one, who from her ancient throne
Leans over, and ends disputations with
Just scales. Show this face, royal ghost,

Rure; breuísque hortus, cuius cum vellere florum
Luctatur spacium, qualem tamen eligit aequi
Iudicij dominus, flores vt iunctiùs halent   25
Stipati, rudibúsque volis imperuius hortus
Sit quasi fasciculus crescens, & nidus odorum.
Hìc ego túque erimus, variae suffitibus herbae
Quotidie pasti: tantùm verum indue vultum
Affectûsque mei similem; nec languida misce   30
Ora meae memori menti: ne dispare cultu
Pugnaces, teneros florum turbemus odores,
Atque inter reliquos horti crescentia foetus
Nostra etiam paribus marcescant gaudia fatis.

And I with you the last of life
Will expend. Without a whisper
Of complaint, I, in person, will hitch
To your chariot alone the Sun's
Team of horses. I grow weak as I
Press my studies—but that the days
In vanity have gone, I will make no moan,
No entombed Minerva whine for,
No hopes that went too far. I will count
My crude imaginings the sterile world's mistake,
To which I leave its pallid stars and comets
As if it had a right to them. Out in the country
I have a tiny house with a panelled ceiling,
Ten roof beams in it; I have
A little garden too, where space
Fights it out with flowers' fleece; still, it is
The kind a tasteful owner wants,
In order to obtain by it
A crowding in of flowers' breathing,
A better harmony of such;
And closed to graceless feet it's like
A posy budding forth, a nest
Of sweet odors. Here you shall be, and I,
Every day on perfumes banqueted—
The smells of many herbs. Just
Wear your real face, one like
The way I feel; do not listless
Mix with my memory your face.
If with polar looks we come
To disagreement, we will break
The fragile flower odors, and among the other
Blossoms budding, our joys linked in fate
Will dissolve in grief away.

VIII.

Paruam piámque dum lubenter semitam
   Grandi reaéque praefero,
Carpsit malignum sydus hanc modestiam
   Vinúmque felle miscuit.
Hinc fremere totus & minari gestio   5
   Ipsis seuerus orbibus;
Tandem prehensâ comiter lacernulâ
   Susurrat aure quispiam,
Haec fuerat olim potio Domini tui.
   Gusto probóque Dolium.   10

IX.

Hoc, Genitrix, scriptum proles tibi sedula mittit.
   Siste parum cantus, dum legis ista, tuos.
Nôsse sui quid agant, quaedam est quoque musica sanctis,
   Quaéque olim fuerat cura, manere potest.
Nos miserè flemus, solésque obducimus almos   5
   Occiduis, tanquam duplice nube, genis.
Interea classem magnis Rex instruit ausis:
   Nos autem flemus: res ea sola tuis.
Ecce solutura est, ventos causata morantes:
   Sin pluuiam, fletus suppeditâsset aquas.   10
Tillius incumbit Dano, Gallúsque marinis,
   Nos flendo: haec nostrûm tessera sola ducum.

8.

I wanted but a tiny way
In virtue, not a grand
Way in guilt: but a star
In wickedness this meekness
Reviled in me, my wine
Mixed with gall. Now all my being
Burns to threaten and to shout,
My eyes themselves turn hard.
Then sweetly in my ear
Someone whispers, my coat
Caught tight by him: "Your Lord
Once had this potion." I taste
And approve the cask.

9.

Your zealous child sends
These verses to you, Mother.
Lay your singing by a bit
As you read them. It is
Music to the very saints
To find out how their kinsmen do,
And what once was their concern
Is able to abide. We weep
And mourn, and suns which make
Things grow, we hood with tears, as with
Twin clouds. While this is going on,
The king equips a fleet for great
Enterprise. Yet we weep:

Sic aeuum exigitur tardum, dum praepetis anni
    Mille rotae nimijs impediuntur aquis.
Plura tibi missurus eram (nam quae mihi laurus,   15
    Quod nectar, nisi cum te celebrare diem?)
Sed partem in scriptis etiam dum lacryma poscit,
    Diluit oppositas candidus humor aquas.

X.

Nempe huc vsque notos tenebricosos
Et maestum nimio madore Caelum
Tellurísque Britannicae saliuam
Iniustè satìs arguit viator.
At te commoriente, Magna Mater,   5
Rectè, quem trahit, aerem repellit

This is for those you rule
The only labor. Look now, the fleet,
That said the wind delayed it,
Shakes out its sails:
If it said rain delayed it,
Tears would have built its tide.
Tilly⁵ pursues the Danes,
The French pursue the sea; we
Pursue tears. Those royal with us
Have only these for code and sign
Among themselves. So slack time is spent,
The quick year's countless wheels
Submerged in immoderate waters.
Many things I almost sent you
(For how can there be laurels for me,
How nectar, unless with you
I pass the day in song?);
But tears insist they be
Included in my verse:
While they do that, a gleaming liquid
Blots affliction's ink.

10.

In truth, up to this time,
The traveler without call
Has been irritated with
The lightless southern wind,
The sky, dark with incessant rain,
And the muddy English ground.
But, royal Mother, with reason at your death

Cum probro madidum, reúmque difflat.
Nam te nunc Ager, Vrbs, & Aula plorant:
Te nunc Anglia, Scotiaéque binae,
Quin te Cambria peruetusta deflet,   10
Deducens lacrymas prioris aeui
Ne serae meritis tuis venirent.
Non est angulus vspiam serenus,
Nec cingit mare, nunc inundat omnes.

XI.

Dum librata suis haeret radicibus ilex
    Nescia vulturnis cedere, firma manet.
Post vbi crudelem sentit diuisa securem,
    Quò placet oblato, mortua fertur, hero:
Arbor & ipse inuersa vocer: dúmque insitus almae   5
    Assideo Matri, robore vinco cedros.
Nunc sorti pateo, expositus sine matre procellis,
    Lubricus, & superans mobilitate salum.
Tu radix, tu petra mihi firmissima, Mater,
    Ceu Polypus, chelis saxa prehendo tenax: 10
Non tibi nunc soli filum abrupere sorores,
    Dissutus videor funere & ipse tuo.
Vnde vagans passim rectè vocer alter Vlysses,
    Alteráque haec tua mors, Ilias esto mihi.

He breathes, swearing, the damp air out
Which he breathes in,
And blows away the culprit. Today lament
Field, court, and city for you;
Today do England, Ireland,
Scotland mourn you; ancient
Wales itself laments for you,
Weeping a former era's tears
So they may come for you
To mourn your excellence in time.
Nowhere a nook of silence now;
The sea's no more a girdle round us, but now
Pours over every man.

11.

The well-poised oak remains strong and fixed,
Unbinding nothing to the wind,
As long as it holds tight to its root.
Later when, split, it feels the savage axe,
That time when its superior has come,
It is, dead, carted off.
I would be known for tree cut down,
Though, when grafted to my mother's richness
I cleave to her, I am more vigorous than cedars.
Now bare to chance, without a mother,
To storms defenseless, mercurial,
More fluid than the open sea, am I.
Root and staunchest rock you are to me, my mother;
I am as polyps, fixed by tentacles to rocks.
The Fates haven't cut your thread alone now,

XII.

Facesse, Stoica plebs, obambulans cautes,
Exuta strato carnis, ossibus constans,
Iísque siccis adeò vt os Molossorum
Haud glubat inde tres teruncios escae.
Dolere prohibes? aut dolere me gentis   5
Adeò inficetae, plumbeae, Meduseae,
Ad saxa speciem retrahentis humanam,
Tantóque nequioris optimâ Pirrhâ?
At fortè matrem perdere haud soles demens:
Quin nec potes; cui praebuit Tigris partum.   10
Proinde parco belluis, nec irascor.

XIII. *Epitaphium*

Hic sita foeminei laus & victoria sexus:
    Virgo pudens, vxor fida, seuera parens:

But by your death I am unraveled too.
So here and there I go about,
And should by right be called another
Ulysses; let this death of yours as well
Be to me another Iliad.

12.

Go, Stoic herd, banging
Into rocks, no flesh for clothes,
All bones, and they so brittle
No Molossian hound[6] could tear
A fraction of a dinner off.
Do you say I may not be sad,
Or tell me I may not lament
For such a graceless progeny—
Leaden, Medusa-like,
Making humans stone, and more
Vain by that than Pyrrha[7] was,
Most worthy Pyrrha? But then again
It may not be to your crazy taste to bring
Catastrophe upon a mother.
You cannot anyway: the Tigris[8]
Gave you birth, and so from tigresses
I keep away, and keep my temper.

13. *Epitaph*

Here the triumph and the glory
Of womanhood: here does she lie—

Magnatúmque inopúmque aequum certamen & ardor:
  Nobilitate illos, hos pietate rapit.
Sic excelsa humilísque simul loca dissita iunxit,   5
  Quicquid habet tellus, quicquid & astra, fruens.

XIV.

Ψυχῆς ἀσθενὲς ἕρκος, ἀμαυρὸν πνεύματος ἄγγος,
  Τῷδε παρὰ τύμβῳ δίζεο, φίλε, μόνον.
Νοῦ δ' αὐτοῦ τάφος ἐστ' ἀστήρ· φέγγος γὰρ ἐκείνου
  Φεγγώδη μόνον, ὡς εἰκός, ἔπαυλιν ἔχει.
Νῦν ὁράᾳς, ὅτι κάλλος ἀπείριτον ὠπὸς ἀπαυγοῦς   5
  Οὐ σαθρόν, οὐδὲ μελῶν ἔπλετο, ἀλλὰ νόος·
Ὃς διὰ σωματίου πρότερον καὶ νῦν δι' Ὀλύμπου
  Ἀστράπτων, θυρίδων ὡς δία, νεῖμε σέλας.

XV.

Μῆτερ, γυναικῶν αἴγλη, ἀνθρώπων ἔρις,
Ὄδυρμα Δαιμόνων, Θεοῦ γεώργιον,
Πῶς νῦν ἀφίπτασαι, γόου καὶ κινδύνου
Ἡμᾶς λιποῦσα κυκλόθεν μεταιχμίους;

Modest virgin, faithful wife,
Strict mother; the fiery contention
Of lord and commoner alike,
The first her dignity attracting,
Her holiness the second. Proud
And meek at once, she unlinked
Regions linked: she took her joy
In earth's possessions, and in the stars'.

14.

The soul's weak wall alone, the spirit's
Blind urn, my friend, seek at this grave—
The mind's tomb is a star, the mind's
Light can only have a house of light,
As it is fitting. You now observe the boundless
Beauty of her brilliant face
Was not mutable—was of the mind,
Not of the flesh. This mind sheds its light,
Flashing through heaven now, as through a window,
That once through her beloved body flashed.

15.

Mother, woman's glory, man's
Contention, devils' cry,
Tilled field of the Lord,
Why do you flee, leaving us
Fenced about by cries,

Μενοῦνγε σοφίην, εἰ σ᾽ ἀπηλλάχθαι χρεών,　　5
Ζωῆς ξυνεργὸν τήνδε διαθεῖναι τέκνοις
Ἐχρῆν φυγοῦσα, τήν τ᾽ ἐπιστήμην βίου.
Μενοῦν τὸ γλαφυρόν, καὶ μελίρροον τρόπων,
Λόγων τε φίλτρον, ὥσθ᾽ ὑπεξελθεῖν λεών.
Νῦν δ᾽ ᾤχου ἔνθενδ᾽ ὡς στρατὸς νικηφόρος　　10
Φέρων τὸ πᾶν, κἄγων· ἢ ὡς Ἀπαρκτίας
Κήπου συνωθῶν ἀνθινὴν εὐωδίαν,
Μίαν τ᾽ ἀταρπὸν συμπορεύεσθαι δράσας.
Ἐγὼ δὲ ῥινὶ ξυμβαλὼν ἰχνηλατῶ
Εἴ που τύχοιμι τῆσδ᾽ ἀρίστης ἀτραποῦ,　　15
Θανεῖν συνειδὼς κρεῖττον, ἢ ἄλλως βιοῦν.

XVI.

Χαλεπὸν δοκεῖ δακρῦσαι,
Χαλεπὸν μὲν οὐ δακρῦσαι·
Χαλεπώτερον δὲ πάντων
Δακρύοντας ἀμπαύεσθαι.
Γενέτειραν οὔ τις ἀνδρῶν　　5
Διδύμαις κόραις τοιαύτην
Ἐποδύρεται πρεπόντως.
Τάλας, εἴθε γ᾽ Ἄργος εἴην
Πολυόμματος, πολύτλας,
Ἵνα μητρὸς εὐθενούσης　　10
Ἀρετὰς διακριθείσας
Ἰδίαις κόραισι κλαύσω.

By perils? Instead, taking flight,
You should have given us, your children
(If you had to go from us), insight
Into life, and wisdom—
These aids in living on; instead
You should have left us manners' smooth
Mellifluous gift, the charm of words
To beat the lion back from us.
But as it was you went from here,
Resistless army, bearing all the plunder off,
Or like the North Wind, compressing the garden's
Ripe smells to a single passage.
I'm on the track, smelling out
Where this best of passages may be,
Sure that death is better than a life in vain.

16.

It's hard to weep it seems, hard
Not to weep, but hardest for those
Who weep to put an end to it.
No man can mourn for such a mother
In a fitting way with his two eyes.
May I, bereaved, be many-eyed
As Argus, and full of many griefs,
So I may mourn with my two eyes
My flowering mother's lofty virtues.

XVII.

Αἰάζω γενέτειραν, ἐπαιάζουσι καὶ ἄλλοι,
Οὐκ ἔτ' ἐμὴν ἰδίας φυλῆς γράψαντες ἀρωγόν,
Προυνομίῳ δ' ἀρετῆς κοινὴν γενέτειραν ἑλόντες.
Οὐκ ἔνι θαῦμα τόσον σφετερίζειν· οὐδὲ γὰρ ὕδωρ,
Οὐ φέγγος, κοινόν τ' ἀγαθόν, μίαν εἰς θύραν εἴργειν
Ἡ θέμις, ἢ δυνατόν. σεμνώματος ἔπλετο στάθμη,   5
Δημόσιόν τ' ἴνδαλμα καλοῦ, θεῖόν τε κάτοπτρον.

Αἰάζω γενέτειραν, ἐπαιάζουσι γυναῖκες,
Οὐκ ἔτι βαλλομένης χάρισιν βεβολημέναι ἦτορ,
Αὗταρ ἄχει μεγάλῳ κεντούμεναι· εὗτε γὰρ αὗται   10
Τῆς περὶ συλλαλέουσιν, ἑοῦ ποικίλματος ἄρδην
Λήσμονες, ἡ βελόνη σφαλερῷ κῆρ τραύματι νύττει
Ἔργου ἁμαρτηκυῖα, νέον πέπλον αἵματι στικτὸν
Μητέρι τεκταίνουσα, γόῳ καὶ πένθεσι σύγχρουν.

Αἰάζω γενέτειραν, ἐπαιάζουσιν ὀπῶραι,   15
Οὐκ ἔτι δεσποίνης γλυκερᾷ μελεδῶνι τραφεῖσαι·
Ἧς βίος ἠελίοιο δίκην, ἀκτῖνας ἱέντος
Πραεῖς εἰαρινούς τε χαραῖς ἐπικίδνατο κῆπον·
Αὗταρ ὅδ' αὖ θάνατος κυρίης, ὡς ἥλιος αὖος
Σειρίου ἡττηθεὶς βουλήμασι, πάντα μαραίνει.   20
Ζῶ δ' αὐτός, βραχύ τι πνείων, ὥστ' ἔμπαλιν αὐτῆς
Αἶνον ὁμοῦ ζώειν καὶ πνεύματος ἄλλο γενέσθαι
Πνεῦμα, βίου πάροδον μούνοις ἐπέεσσι μετρῆσαν.

17.

I mourn my mother, as well as other men
Who do not make her now my clan's
Especial guardian, but, since she was virtuous,
Want her for their own mother.
It isn't very strange they claim her,
For it isn't right or possible to keep
Behind a single door the common blessings
Of water or of light. She was the purest law,
Beauty's vision to the world, the glass of God.

I mourn my mother, as well as women
Who do not warmly take to heart her love's
Arrows now, but have their grief to pierce them.
For while they talk of her among themselves,
Forgetting their embroidery, their needles, off
The mark, and wounding by mistake, prick
Their hearts, for my mother fashioning
A special gown, a print of blood on it, dyed
The same as grief and lamentation are.

I mourn my mother, as well as fruits and flowers,
Which are not taken care of by their mistress'
Sweet attention now—her whose presence did,
As would the sun with soft and mild beams,
Overspread the garden with delights.
For now the mistress' death—as would the sun
Dried up, beaten by the Dog Star's schemes—
Shrivels all. And yet I live, though weak
Of breath, to compensate for which her praise
Lives in me, breath of my breath, counting
Out the passage of her life by words alone.

XVIII.

Κύματ᾿ ἐπαφριοῶντα Θαμήσεος, αἴκε σελήνης
   Φωτὸς ἀπαυραμένης ὄγκου ἐφεῖσθε πλέον,
Νῦν θέμις ὀρφναίῃ μεγάλης ἐπὶ γείτονος αἴσῃ
   Οὐλυμπόνδε βιβᾶν ὔμμιν ἀνισταμένοις.
᾿Αλλὰ μενεῖτ᾿, οὐ γὰρ τάραχος ποτὶ μητέρα βαίνῃ,   5
   Καὶ πρέπον ὧδε παρὰ δακρυόεσσι ῥέειν.

XIX.

Excussos manibus calamos, falcémque resumptam
   Rure, sibi dixit Musa fuisse probro.
Aggreditur Matrem (conductis carmine Parcis)
   Funeréque hoc cultum vindicat aegra suum.
Non potui non ire acri stimulante flagello: 5
   Quin Matris superans carmina poscit honos.
Eia, agedum scribo: vicisti, Musa; sed audi,
   Stulta: semel scribo, perpetuò vt sileam.

18.

Whitecaps of Thames, if you would rob the moon
Of light—take more of her burden up—
Rise up upon the darkened shore
Of your great neighbor, and rush to heaven!
No, wait! No tumult should approach my mother:
In darkness you should flow by us who weep.

19.

The Muse has made it known
The laying down of quills from hands,
The taking up again of scythes in fields,
Have been discourtesy to her.
She to my mother goes (the Fates
By song bought off) and by this death
Grown ill, claims her own
Kind of worship there. I could not stay
Away: her flagellation drove me.
More, my mother's excellence, her honor,
Must needs be sung to. Well then, I write.
Muse, you win. But hear,
O vain one! This one time I write
To be forever still.

Alia Poemata Latina

In Obitum Henrici Principis Walliae

Ite leues (inquam), Parnassia numina, Musae,
Non ego vos posthâc hederae velatus amictu
Somnis (nescio queîs) nocturna ad vota vocabo:
Sed nec Cyrrhaei saltus Libethriáue arua
In mea dicta ruant; non tam mihi pendula mens est,   5
Sic quasi Dijs certem, magnos accersere montes:
Nec vaga de summo deducam flumina monte,
Qualia parturiente colunt sub rupe sorores:
Si-quas mens agitet moles (dum pectora saeuo
Tota stupent luctu) lachrymísque exaestuet aequis   10
Spiritus, hi mihi iam montes, haec flumina sunto.
Musa, vale, & tu Phoebe; dolor mea carmina dictet;
Hinc mihi principium: vos o labentia mentis
Lumina, nutantes paulatim acquirite vires,
Viuite, dum mortem ostendam: sic tempora vestram   15
Non comedant famam, sic nulla obliuia potent.
Quare age, Mens, effare, precor, quo numine laeso?
Quae suberant causae? quid nos committere tantum,

Other Latin Poems

On the death of Henry, the Prince of Wales[1]

Airy Muses, powers of poetry, go,
I say: I will no longer, cloaked in ivy,
Summon you from dreams to midnight worship.
I do not ask that Cirrha's clearings, Libethra's[2]
Tilled fields hasten to my words.
I'm not in the mood to call
Huge mountains near, as if I were
At war with all the gods. I will not pull
The crooked waters from the mountain heights,
The sort of water which the Muses tend
Beneath the oozing cliff. If my intellect must labor
With insupportable burdens (while all my heart
Is stricken by pitiless grief), and my spirit boil
With tears to equal them, let these now become
My mountains, become my streams.
Muse, and also Phoebus, goodbye: let sorrow
Tell me what to sing. Thus will I begin:
O straying eyes of intellect, slowly
Accumulate a timid strength, live
While I portray a death. In this way time

Quod non Lanigerae pecudes, non Agmina lustrent?
Annon longa fames miseraéque iniuria pestis   20
Poena minor fuerat, quàm fatum Principis aegrum?
Iam foelix Philomela, & menti conscia Dido!
Foelices, quos bella premunt, & plurimus ensis!
Non metuunt vltrà; nostra infortunia tantùm
Fatáque Fortunásque & spem laesêre futuram.   25
Quòd si fata illi longam invidêre salutem
Et patrio regno (sub quo iam Principe nobis
Quid sperare, imò quid non sperare licebat?)
Debuit ista pati prima & non noblis aetas:
Aut cita mors est danda bonis aut longa senectus: 30
Sic lactare animos & sic ostendere gemmam
Excitat optatus auidos, & ventilat ignem.
Quare etiam nuper Pyrij de pulueris ictu
Principis innocuam seruastis numina Vitam,
Vt morbi perimant, alióque in puluere prostet?   35
Phoebe, tui puduit quum summo manè redires
Sol sine sole tuo! quàm te tum nubibus atris
Totum offuscari peteres, vt nocte silenti
Humana aeternos agerent praecordia questus:
Tantùm etenim vestras (Parcae) non flectit habenas   40
Tempus edax rerum, túque o mors improba sola es,
Cui caecas tribuit vires annosa vetustas.
Quid non mutatum est? requiêrunt flumina cursus;
Plus etiam veteres coelum videre remotum:
Cur ideo verbis tristes effundere curas   45
Expeto, tanquam haec sit nostri medicina doloris?
Immodicus luctus tacito vorat igne medullas,
Vt, fluuio currente, vadum sonat, alta quiescunt.

Will not eat up your fame; in this way
No lapse of memory can do it. And so awaken,
Intellect, divulge, I ask you, what it was
That gave offense to God, what the underlying reasons
    were,
What sin on our part was so great
No beast of wool, no stream could cleanse it?
Would not have famine or the plague's bleak
Visitation been a lesser punishment
Than the Prince's painful fate? Now Philomel[3] is blessed,
And Dido also, conscious of her future act.
Those oppressed by war and the many-bladed sword
Are lucky! They fear no more. Our misfortunes only
Have wounded fate and luck and future hope.
But if the Fates were miserly with enduring
Security to him and the kingdom of his fathers
(And now as subjects of the Prince, what blessings
We could have waited for! Indeed what
Blessings could we not have waited for?),
The unrenowned, initial age of life
Should have been struck: instant death
Or long old age is what the good deserve.
To delude the mind with hollow hopes this way,
To show the jewel thus, kindles the greedy wish
And blows upon the flame. Why too of late, O God,
Did you preserve the Prince's life unscathed
From the shock of burning dust,[4] in order that disease
Might snuff it out, in order that he might
Be demonstrated in another dust?
Phoebus, you were mortified when you, the sun,
At break of day came back without your sun.
How then you might have begged that you be all
Covered over in black clouds, so human hearts

Innupta Pallas, nata Diespitre,
Aeterna summae gloria regiae,
    Cui dulcis arrident Camoenae
        Pieridis Latiaéque Musae,

Cur tela Mortis vel tibi vel tuis   5
Quâcunque guttâ temporis imminent?
    Tantâque propendet staterâ
        Regula sanguinolenta fati?

Númne Hydra talis, tantáne bellua est
Mors tot virorum sordida sanguine,   10
    Vt mucro rumpatur Mineruae,
        Vtque minax superetur Aegis?

Might make eternal lamentations
In soundless night! O Fates, your reins alone
Time the glutton does not bend, and you, O
Evil Death, are the only one that ripe old age
Has left blind power to. Is anything the same?
The streams have quieted their rapid ways;
Men of old saw heaven even farther off.
Why then do I attempt to spill from me in words
Dolorous concerns, as though for all our misery
This were the medicine? In soundless fire
Immoderate lamentation eats the heart,
Just as when a river flows, the shallows
Cry, and the depths are still.

Virgin Pallas, Zeus's daughter,
Eternal glory of heaven's house,
For whom Latium's and sweet
Pieria's spirits laugh,
Why at every tick of time
Do Death's arrows poise above
You and yours, and Fate's bloody
Judgment hover over you with such
Ponderous scales? Surely Hydra can't
Be such a beast, and Death, filthed
By the blood of multitudes
Be so strong a beast Minerva's
Sword tip is shivered to pieces, the Aegis' threat
Brought to nothing. You detour rivers;
They say you burned the azure sea
With a plummeting thunderbolt,
Tumbling down the eaten triremes

Tu flectis amnes, tu mare caerulum
Vssisse prono fulmine diceris,
    Aiacis exesas triremes   15
        Praecipitans grauiore casu.

Tu discidisti Gorgoneas manus
Nexas, capillos anguibus oblitos,
    Furuósque vicisti Gigantes,
        Enceladum pharetrámque Rhoeci.   20

Ceu victa, Musis porrigit herbulas
Pennata caeci dextra Cupidinis,
    Non vlla Bellonae furentis
        Arma tui metuunt alumni.

Pallas retortis caesia vocibus   25
Respondit: Eia, ne metuas, precor,
    Nam fata non iustis repugnant
        Principibus, sed amica fiunt.

Vt si recisis arboribus meis
Nudetur illic lucus amabilis,   30
    Fructúsque post mortem recusent
        Perpetuos mihi ferre rami,

Dulcem rependent tum mihi tibiam
Pulchrè renatam ex arbore mortuâ,
    Dignámque coelesti coronâ   35
        Harmoniam dabit inter astra.

Of Ajax. You've cut off
Gorgon's shackled hands, her snake-
Smeared hair, and beaten
The black giants, Enceladus and
Rhoetus with his quiver.[5] As if beaten,
Blind Cupid's feathered right hand
Holds out little herbs to the Muses;
Your followers are not afraid of any
Of raging Bellona's armaments.

Grey-eyed Pallas answers back
With flying words: Ai, don't be
Frightened, I beg you, for the Fates
Are not against impartial princes,
But become their intimates.
If, my trees depleted,
My handsome grove's denuded there,
And the branches after death
Won't make eternal fruit for me,
They will give me in return the sweet
Tibia, exquisitely fashioned anew
From the dead trees, and give to me,
Fit for heaven's diadem,
A tune among the Stars.

In Natales et Pascha
Concurrentes

Cum tu, Christe, cadis, nascor; mentémque ligauit
    Vna meam membris horula, téque cruci.
O me disparibus natum cum numine fatis!
    Cur mihi das vitam, quam tibi, Christe, negas?
Quin moriar tecum: vitam, quam negligis ipse,   5
    Accipe; ni talem des, tibi qualis erat.
Hoc mihi legatum tristi si funere praestes,
    Christe, duplex fiet mors tua vita mihi:
Atque vbi per te sanctificer natalibus ipsis,
    In vitam & neruos Pascha coaeua fluet.   10

In Obitum Serenissimae Reginae Annae

Quo Te, foelix Anna, modo deflere licebit?
    Cui magnum imperium, gloria maior erat:
Ecce meus torpens animus succumbit vtrique,
    Cui tenuis fama est, ingeniúmque minus.
Quis, nisi qui manibus Briareus, oculísque sit Argus,   5
    Scribere, Te dignùm, vel lachrymare queat!

On the concurrence of a birthday and Good Friday [6]

Christ, when you die, I am born.
One little hour fixed
My intellect to limbs, you to the Cross.
O me, born with a fate
So unlike God's! Christ, why give me
The life which you deny yourself?
Surely I will die with you: take up the life
That you yourself pay no attention to—
Unless the kind you give is
The kind you had.
If you bequeath it, Christ, to me
By your doleful death, that death to me
Will turn to double life:
When I am sanctified through you
On my very day of birth, Good Friday then,
Just as old as I, will flow
Into every fibre of my being.

On the death of fairest Queen Anne [7]

How is it permissible, blessed Anne,
To weep for you, you who possessed
Great government, and greater glory?
See, my fading spirit falls before both,
For I have little power, and less ability.
Only if I had Briareus' [8] hands
Or Argus' eyes would I be capable

Frustra igitur sudo: superest mihi sola voluptas,
  Quòd calamum excusent Pontus & Astra meum:
Namque Annae laudes coelo scribuntur aperto,
  Sed luctus noster scribitur Oceano.   10

Ad Autorem Instaurationis Magnae

Per strages licet autorum veterúmque ruinam
  Ad famae properes vera Tropaea tuae,
Tam nitidè tamen occidis, tam suauiter, hostes,
  Se quasi donatum funere quisque putat.
Scilicet apponit pretium tua dextera fato,   5
  Vulneréque emanat sanguis, vt intret honos.
O quàm felices sunt, qui tua castra sequuntur,
  Cùm per te sit res ambitiosa mori.

Comparatio inter Munus
Summi Cancellariatus et Librum

Munere dum nobis prodes, Libróque futuris,
  In laudes abeunt secula quaeque tuas;
Munere dum nobis prodes, Libróque remotis,
  In laudes abeunt iam loca quaeque tuas:
Hae tibi sunt alae laudum. Cui contigit vnquam   5
  Longius aeterno, latius orbe decus?

Of tears and phrases worthy of you.
And so I labor fruitlessly.
The only pleasure left for me is this:
The sea and stars excuse my ink—
For Anne's praises are inscribed
In the clear heavens, while in the ocean
My lamentations have their wording.

To the author of Instauratio Magna [9]

Although through ancient authors' wrack and ruin
You hurry to your fame's true rewards,
Still with so much charm and wit you slay your foes,
Each one considers, as it were, death a gift for him.
Your right hand surely sweetens fate, and blood
Issues from the wound to make a way for honor.
Your followers are very lucky,
For in your service death's a kingly thing.

Comparison between the office and the book of the High Chancellor [10]

While you give aid to us who live today
By means of your position, to those who live tomorrow
By virtue of your book, all times praise you.
While you give aid to us who live right here
By means of your position, to those who live far off
By virtue of your book, all places praise you.
These make up the wings of your encomiums.

In Honorem Illustr. D.D. Verulamij, S^{ti} Albani, Mag. Sigilli Custodis post editam ab eo Instaurationem Magnam

Quis iste tandem? non enim vultu ambulat
Quotidiano! Nescis, ignare? Audies!
Dux Notionum; veritatis Pontifex;
Inductionis Dominus, & Verulamij;
Rerum magister vnicus, at non Artium,   5
Profunditatis pinus, atque Elegantiae;
Naturae Aruspex intimus; Philosophiae
Aerarium; sequester expèrientiae,
Speculationísque; Aequitatis signifer;
Scientiarum, sub pupillari statu   10
Degentium olim, Emancipator; Luminis
Promus; Fugator Idolûm, atque nubium;
Collega Solis; Quadra Certitudinis;
Sophismatomastix; Brutus Literarius,
Authoritatis exuens tyrannidem;   15
Rationis & sensûs stupendus Arbiter;
Repumicator mentis; Atlas Physicus,
Alcide succumbente Stagiritico;
Columba Noae, quae in vetustis artibus
Nullum locum requiémue cernens perstitit   20
Ad se suaéque matris Arcam regredi:
Subtilitatis Terebra; Temporis Nepos

Who else has ever had the good luck of a glory more
Eternal than eternity, and wider than the world?

In honor of the Illustrious Baron Verulam, Viscount St. Alban, Keeper of the Great Seal, after the publication of his Instauratio Magna [11]

Who is he then? For he doesn't go
With a common look about him. Blockhead,
Don't you know? Listen here. He is
The instigator of research, archpriest
Of truth, lord of the inductive method
And of Verulam, unique
Master of factual material,
But not of arts; evergreen of elegance
And of profundity, Nature's cosmographer,
Philosophy's store, trustee
Of speculation and experiment,
Color-bearer of impartiality, savior
Of science, long an orphan now;
Minister of light, bedevilment of idols
And clouds, colleague of the Sun, truth's
Measurer, sophistry's whip, literary
Brutus, casting off the yoke of books,
Sense and reason's miraculous
Discriminator, polisher of intellect,
Atlas of Nature, champion over
The herculean Stagirite;[12] Noah's dove
Which, discovering no place or peace
In ancient arts, was bent on going back
To itself and to its mother's ark;

Ex Veritate matre; Mellis alueus;
Mundíque & Animarum sacerdos vnicus;
Securis errorum; ínque Naturalibus   25
Granum Sinapis, acre Alijs, crescens sibi:
   O me probè lassum! Iuuate, Posteri!

Aethiopissa ambit Cestum
Diuersi Coloris Virum

Quid mihi si facies nigra est? hoc, Ceste, colore
   Sunt etiam tenebrae, quas tamen optat amor.
Cernis vt exustâ semper sit fronte viator;
   Ah longum, quae te deperit, errat iter.
Si nigro sit terra solo, quis despicit aruum?   5
   Claude oculos, & erunt omnia nigra tibi:
Aut aperi, & cernes corpus quas proijcit vmbras;
   Hoc saltem officio fungar amore tui.
Cùm mihi sit facies fumus, quas pectore flammas
   Iamdudum tacitè delituisse putes?   10
Dure, negas? O fata mihi praesaga doloris,
   Quae mihi lugubres contribuere genas!

Subtlety's gimlet, grandson of time
From Mother Truth; hive of honey; world's
And spirit's only priest; error's axe;
Mustard seed within the science of natural things,
Sour to others, flourishing unto itself.
Oh, I'm all worn out. Posterity, take over!

A *negro maid woos Cestus,*
a man of a different color

What do I care if my face is black?
Dark, O Cestus, has this color too, but love
Wants it anyway. You are aware that always
The forehead of the traveler is scorched.
Ah, the girl who perishes for love of you
Has a long way to go. Who despises
The furrow if the land is black? Shut your eyes,
And all you see is black. Open them,
And you will see the shade the body makes.
I will do at least this service
Out of love for you. Because my face is smoke,
What fires do you think have hid within my heart
So long in silence now? O stony man,
Do you say no? O Fates who gave me
Mournful cheeks, fortelling my affliction!

In obitum incomparabilis Francisci
Vicecomitis Sancti Albani, Baronis Verulamij

Dum longi lentíque gemis sub pondere morbi
  Atque haeret dubio tabida vita pede,
Quid voluit prudens Fatum, iam sentio tandem:
  Constat, *Aprile* vno te potuisse mori:
Vt *Flos* hinc lacrymis, illinc *Philomela* querelis,   5
  Deducant *linguae* funera sola tuae.

Dum petit Infantem

Dum petit Infantem Princeps, Grantámque Iacobus,
  Quisnam horum maior sit, dubitatur, amor.
Vincit more suo Noster: nam millibus Infans
  Non tot abest, quot nos Regis ab ingenio.

On the death of the incomparable Francis, Viscount St. Alban, Baron Verulam [13]

While you groan beneath the weight of long-
Drawn-out illness, and with a tottering foot
Life, wasting away, hangs on, I see at last
What discreet destiny has willed: it is
Certain there has never been a choice: April
Has always been the month for you to die in, that here
Flora[14] with her tears, and Philomela there
With her lamentations, may conduct
Your idiom's lonely funeral cortege.

[The following translations are Herbert's.]

While he seeks the Infanta [15]

While Prince to Spaine, and King to Cambridge goes,
The question is, whose loue the greater showes:
Ours (like himselfe) o'recomes; for his wit's more
Remote from ours, then Spaine from Britains shoare.

In Sacram Anchoram Piscatoris G. Herbert

Quod Crux nequibat fixa, Clavíque additi,
(Tenere Christum scilicet, ne ascenderet)
Tuíue Christum deuocans facundia
Vltra loquendi tempus; addit Anchora:
Nec hoc abundè est tibi, nisi certae Anchorae   5
Addas sigillum: nempe Symbolum suae
Tibi debet Vnda & Terra certitudinis.

Munde, fluas fugiásque licet, nos nostráque fixi:
    Deridet motus sancta catena tuos.
    Quondam fessus Amor loquens Amato,   10
    Tot & tanta loquens amica, scripsit:
    Tandem & fessa manus, dedit sigillum.

Suauis erat, qui scripta dolens lacerando recludi,
Sanctius in Regno Magni credebat Amoris
(In quo fas nihil est rumpi) donare sigillum.   15

On the sacred anchor of the fisherman [16]

Although the Crosse could not Christ here detain,
Though nail'd unto't, but he ascends again,
Nor yet thy eloquence here keep him still,
But onely while thou speak'st; This Anchor will.
Nor canst thou be content, unlesse thou to
This certain Anchor adde a Seal, and so
The Water, and the Earth both unto thee
Doe owe the symbole of their certainty.
Let the world reel, we and all ours stand sure,
This holy Cable's of all storms secure.
   When Love being weary made an end
   Of kinde Expressions to his friend,
   He writ; when 's hand could write no more,
   He gave the Seale, and so left o're.
How sweet a friend was he, who being griev'd
His letters were broke rudely up, believ'd
'Twas more secure in great Loves Common-weal
(Where nothing should be broke) to adde a Seal.

ANOTHER VERSION

When my dear Friend, could write no more,
He gave this *Seal*, and, so gave ore.
When winds and waves rise highest, I am sure,
This *Anchor* keeps my *faith*, that, me secure.

Notes

Poems in Response to Andrew Melville's
Con-Oxford-Cambridge Accusations

1. The *Musae Responsoriae* was not published during Herbert's life, but appeared in the *Ecclesiastes Solomonis* (1662) of James Duport, a fellow student with Herbert at Westminster School and later at Trinity College, Cambridge. The *Musae* was written in response to the Scottish religious reformer Andrew Melville's *Anti-Tami-Cami-Categoria*, a long polemical Latin poem in defense of Puritan liturgical usage, and specifically in opposition to Oxford and Cambridge for their negative reaction to the Millenary Petition, which was handed to James on his way to London in behalf of the Puritan clergy of the English Church, and requested that such liturgical usages as the Cross and the questions put to infants in Baptism, the surplice, the biretta and the marriage ring, long services and elaborate songs and music, be abandoned. It also urged that restrictions be placed on bishops.

   That Herbert should involve himself in a public religious controversy may stem partially at least from the fact that in 1618 he became Reader in Rhetoric *(Praelector)* at Cambridge, and in 1619/20 Public Orator there, a position considered a crucial steppingstone to high political position, since the Orator wrote the University's letters and composed and delivered its official welcomes to visiting royalty. In short, Herbert was at this time at the height of his youthful ambition and most in the public eye.

2. Pallas' aegis had a fringe of snakes and a Gorgon's face.

3. Walton (*Lives*) speaks of Herbert's love of music: "His chiefest recreation was Musick, in which heavenly Art he was a most excellent Master, and did himself compose many divine Hymns and Anthems, which he set and sung to his Lute or Viol."

4. *Lucas*, XXV.

5. In the Millenary Petition.

6. Apostolic Succession.

7. From Ovid's *Fasti*, II, 235–6. Herbert uses *Catharos* for *Fabios*.

8. Edinburgh.

9. Those who signed the Millenary Petition.

10. Cymbals were used in the orgiastic worship on Berecynthus in Thessaly.

The Events of the Passion

1. The *Passio Discerpta* was published along with the *Lucus* by Grossart in the *Complete Works in Verse and Prose of George Herbert* in 1874, with the exception of *Triumphus Mortis* in *Lucus,* which was printed as *Inventica Bella* in William Pickering's *Works of George Herbert,* I ("Life and Remains") in 1836. Herbert probably wrote the *Passio* and *Lucus* at the same time, for they are both annexed in the Williams MS. (their primary source) in his own handwriting; he most likely composed them about 1623, as the epigrams on Pope Urban VIII in *Lucus* indicate, since he became pope and assumed his title in August, 1623. That is, Herbert seems to have written them when he was still Public Orator of Cambridge, which he remained until 1627.

The year 1623 marks the height of Herbert's activity at Cambridge; during this year he delivered the three orations still extant. After 1624 he stayed away from the University for the most part, both for the sake of his bad health and perhaps to further his ambition for a more public life. But in 1625 he appears to have been living a retired life: though James I died in this year, Herbert neither delivered the oration on his death at Cambridge nor contributed to the memorial anthology of the University honoring his death. In this year he returned to London and announced his decision to take Orders. In the following year he assisted in compiling the Cambridge memorial anthology honoring the death of Francis Bacon, which includes his own contribution. In the same year he delivered the oration for the installation of the Duke of Buckingham as Chancellor of Cambridge and, again for reasons of health, went to live with his brother Henry in Essex.

In view of his diminishing public activity shortly after 1623, and in view of the fact that both the *Passio Discerpta* and the *Lucus* are largely didactic rather than devotional in the sense of many of his later English poems, it seems reasonable to place them in the earlier phase of Herbert's creative activity.

2. Christ's divine nature.

The Sacred Grove

1. Wife of Philemon. They were an old and poor couple visited by Zeus and Hermes in disguise; for their hospitality their house was turned into a temple and they were made priests to tend it.

2. Quintus Fabius Maximus, appointed dictator by the Romans to deal with Hannibal's successful invasion of Italy, pursued a policy of delaying action.

3. One of the chief Roman Catholic theologians of the Counter-Reformation.

4. Peneus: Battle of Pharsalia, 48 B.C. Daunia: Battle of Cannae where Hannibal defeated the Romans in 216 B.C.

5. Bellona, native to Roman mythology.

6. A king of Macedonia who attacked Rhodes with large war machines.

7. A personification of infernal odors.

8. A giant, the son of Vulcan.

In Sacred Memory of My Mother

1. This group of poems was appended to John Donne's *Sermon of Commemoration of the Lady Danvers* (Herbert's mother), delivered and printed on the occasion of her death in 1627.

    Though the convention of the classical funeral elegy called for the kind of mourning one finds in the *Memoriae*, part of this convention may stem from the fact that during this period (1625–8/9) Herbert was having difficulty becoming adjusted to his choice of the religious life, as some of the autobiographical poems in *The Temple* written about this time indicate.

2. A river in Asia Minor fabled for its golden sands.

3. Daughter of Zeus and Themis, and the last of the gods to leave the earth after the Golden Age. The constellation of the Virgin holding scales.

4. Goddess of divine justice, and the protector of the oppressed and the rights of hospitality.

5. Commander of the army of the Catholic League who defeated Christian IV of Denmark at Lutter in 1626.

6. Wolfhound.

7. Wife of Deucalion. They turned stones into humans after Zeus destroyed mankind with a flood.

8. Diogenes, who popularized Stoicism in Rome, came from Seleucia on the Tigris.

Other Latin Poems

1. Herbert was nineteen when he wrote these two, his first published poems, on the death of Henry Frederick, James I's eldest son, who died in 1619 at the age of nineteen.

2. Cirrha was the ancient port serving Delphi, the seat of the oracle of Apollo, and Libethra, a fountain on Mount Helicon sacred to the Muses.

3. Sister of Procne, Tereus' husband. He raped her and cut out her tongue, and she and Procne served him his son in a meal. When he chased them both, all three turned into birds, Philomel into a nightingale.

4. The Gunpowder Plot.

5. The battle between the gods and giants, in which Heracles assisted the gods and Athena took part.

6. Probably written in 1618 since it reflects Herbert's earlier style. In this year Good Friday fell on Herbert's birthday, April 3.

7. Anne of Denmark, James I's wife, who died in 1618/19.

8. Son of Uranus and Gaea, having a hundred arms and fifty hands (according to Hesiod). After he and his two brothers had aided the gods in their battle against the Titans, all three were set to guard the Titans in Tartarus.

9. Written on the publication in 1620 of the *Novum Organum,* the second part of Bacon's *Instauratio Magna.*

10. Bacon had given his book to Cambridge in 1620.

11. First published in *Caesares,* a collection of Latin verse by the Italian Jesuit Emanuele Tesauro, at Oxford in 1637. Written between Jan. 1620/1 when Bacon was made Viscount St. Alban, and the following May when the Great Seal was taken from him.

12. Aristotle.

13. First appeared in 1626 in the Cambridge memorial anthology on Bacon's death which Herbert helped compile.

14. Roman goddess of flowers.

15. On the visit of Prince Charles (Charles I) to Spain in 1622/3 to woo the Infanta.

16. Herbert apparently wrote these two versions in thanks to John Donne for sending him a seal depicting Christ crucified on an anchor. The first fourteen lines of the English translation of the first version appear in Izaak Walton's life of John Donne.